SPEED-READING FOR VIOLIN

VELOCITY, AGILITY & CONCENTRATION DRILLS

MB21779

BY JOHN BAUER

Visit us on the Web at www.melbay.com or www.billsmusicshelf.com

CONTENTS

Preface

In language, speed reading relies on eye focus, mental focus, and seeing groups of letters, or groups of words, as units. The same priciples apply to music reading.

This book is designed to develop those abilities.

The Appendix gives a detailed guide for how to use the book to develop the 'focus' technics. The recommended procedures take about 15-25 minutes to practice one entry. After one month it is typical for a person to improve 45%. For example: If a person can read a new entry at an mm. setting of 72, one will increase the initial speed to about 104 in one month.

Practicing all of the entries as designed will result in all possible finger patterns being covered, and in all possible combinations of whole steps and half steps.

The Drills

Eventually patterns 1-24 should be practiced in the Major key signatures of C, D, E, F, whole tones, and in semi-tones. Triplets are for augmented seconds.

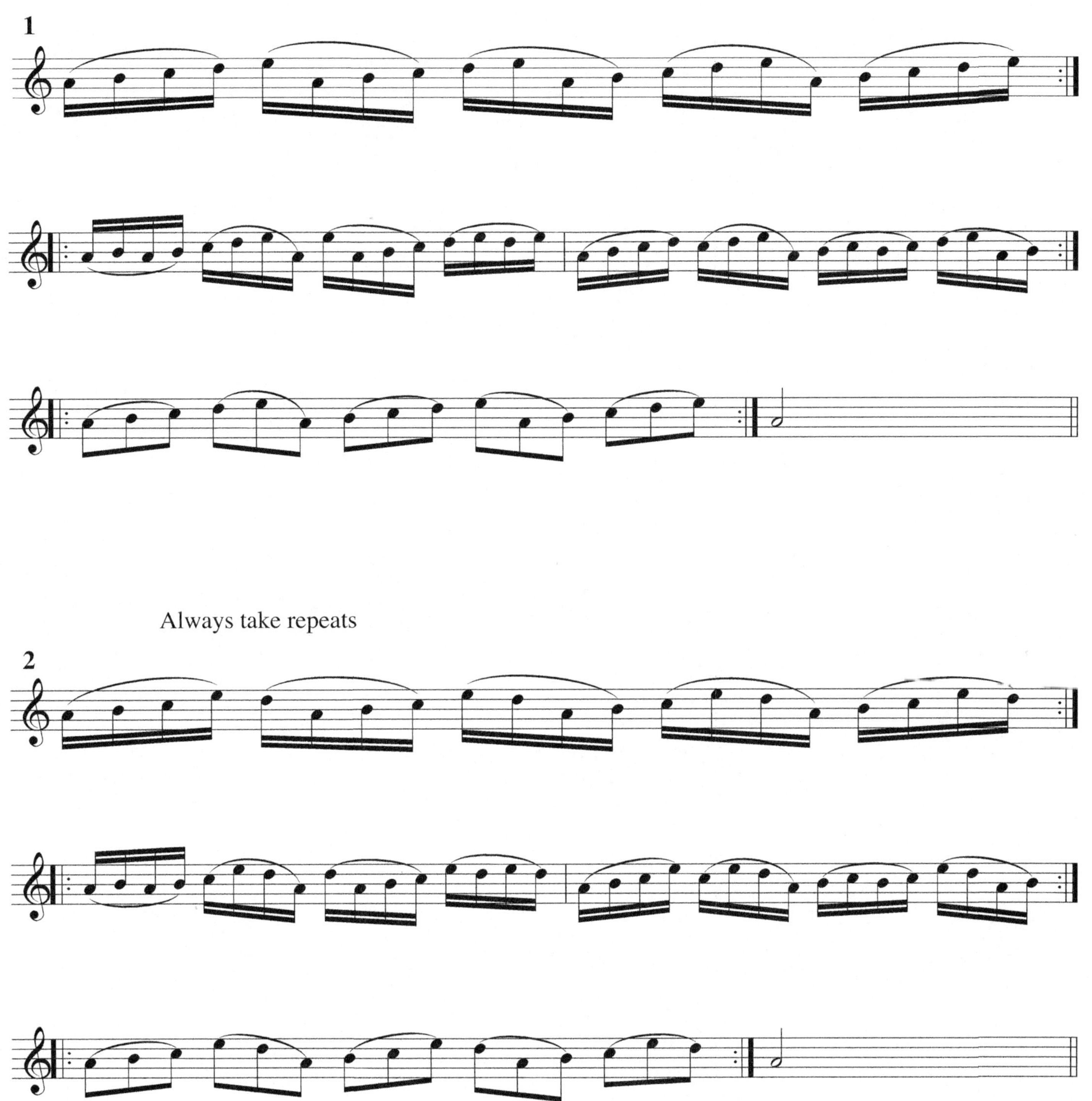

Focus energy in the left fingers...quiet left hand.

5

Retain fingers. See line 2. Apply principle throughout.

6

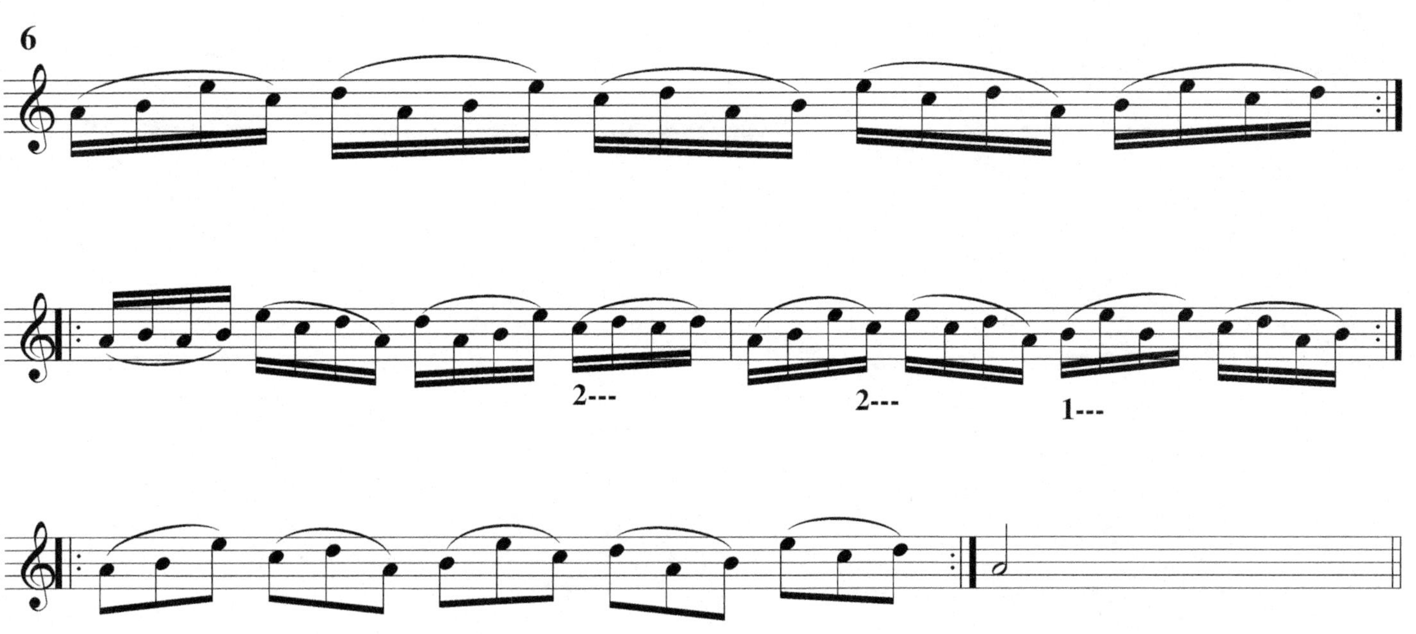

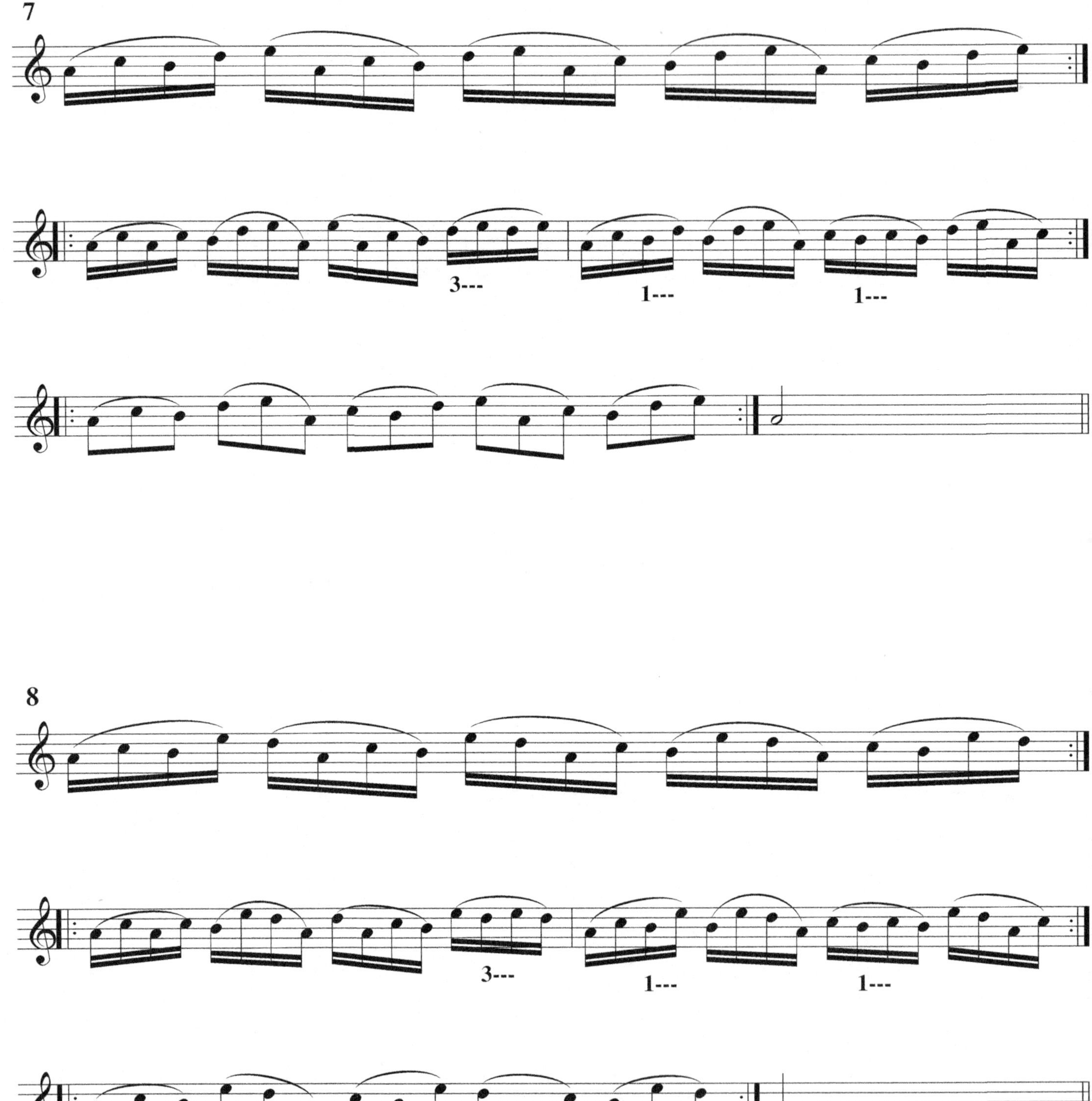

7
3---
1---
1---
8
3---
1---
1---

9

Check left thumb placement

10

"Slap" fingers of the left hand, without tension.

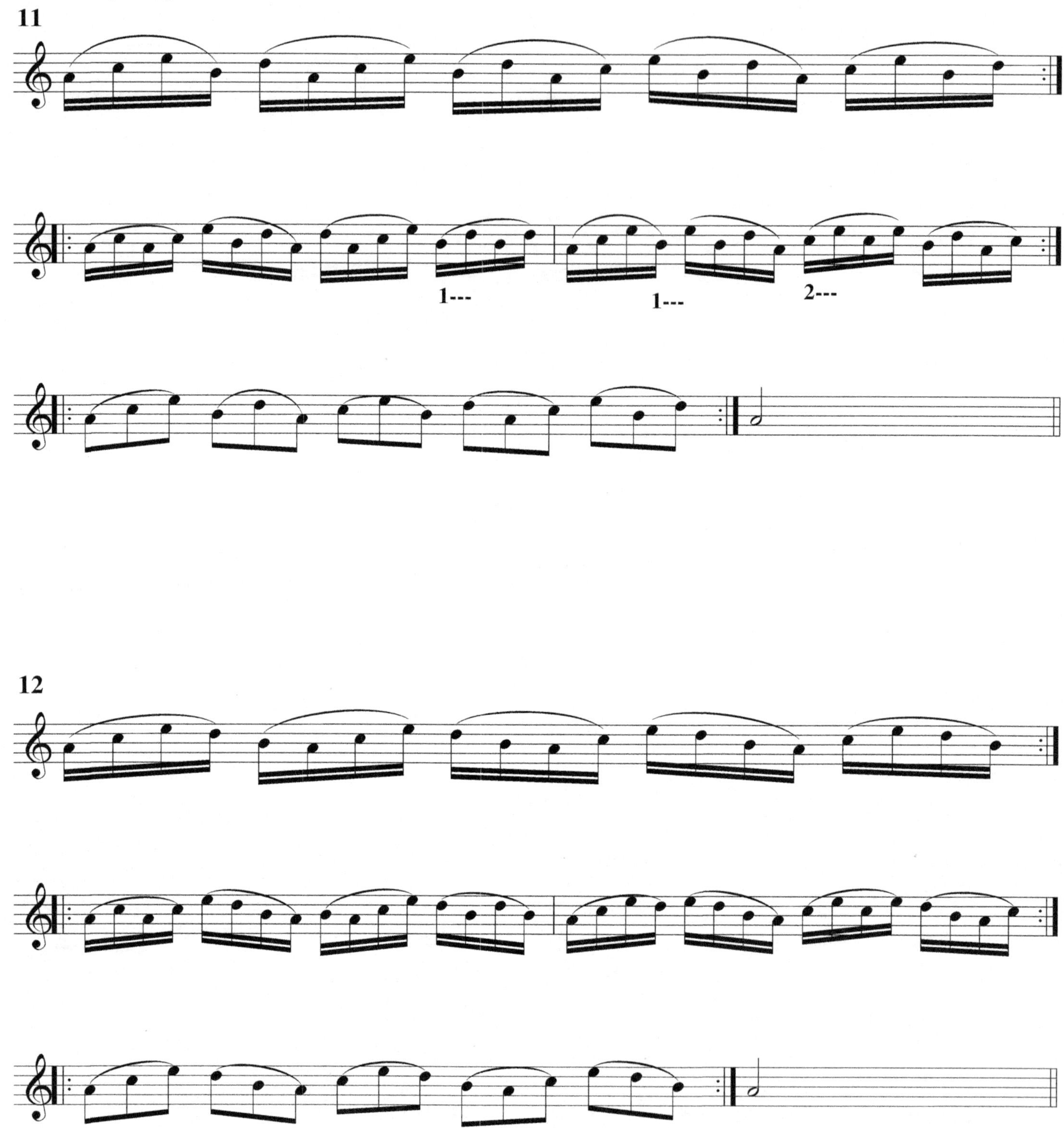

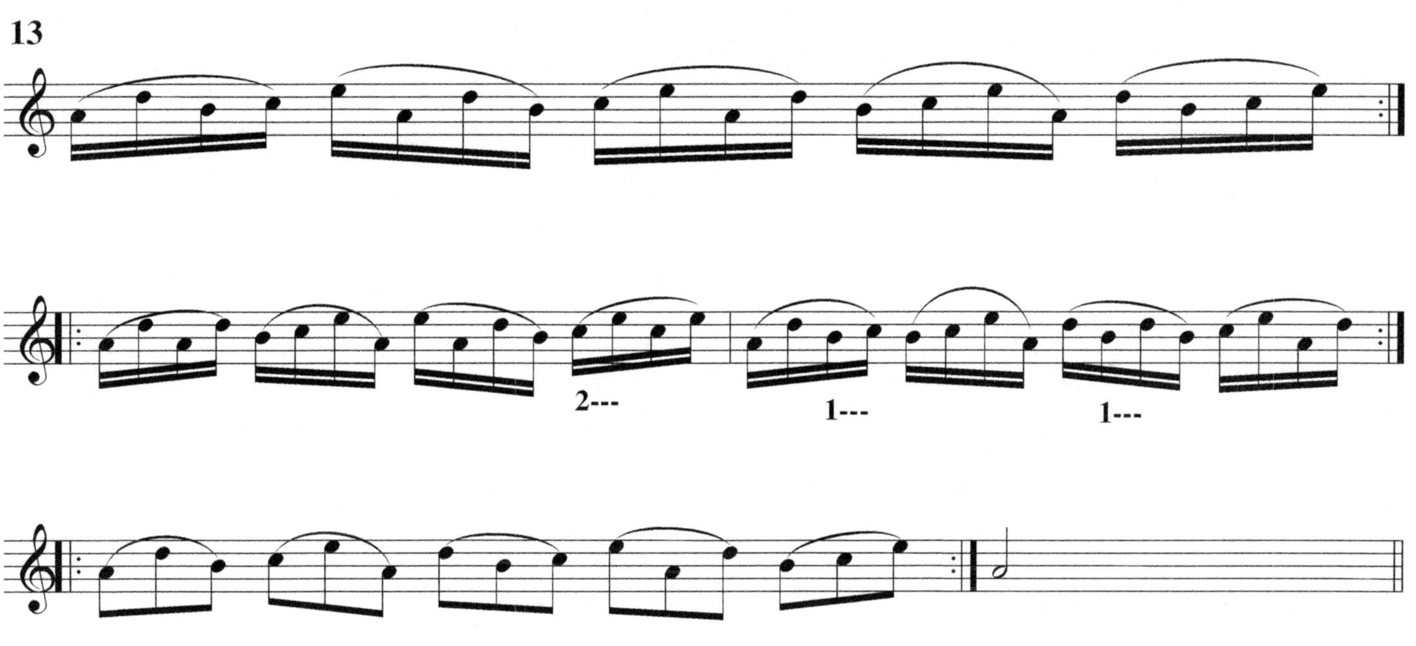

13

Slap high fourth finger.

14

Anticipating finger placement is an element of efficiency.

15

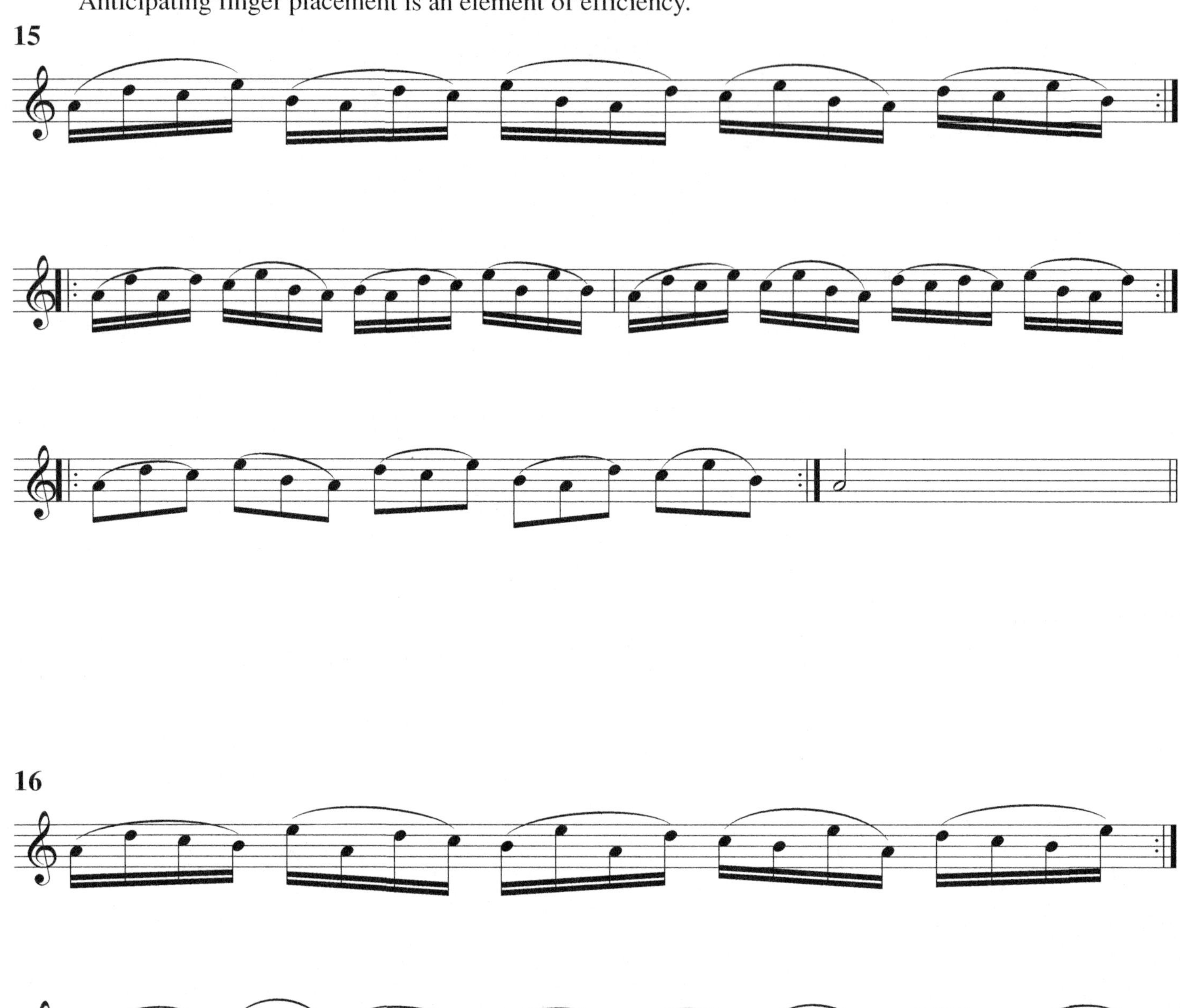

16

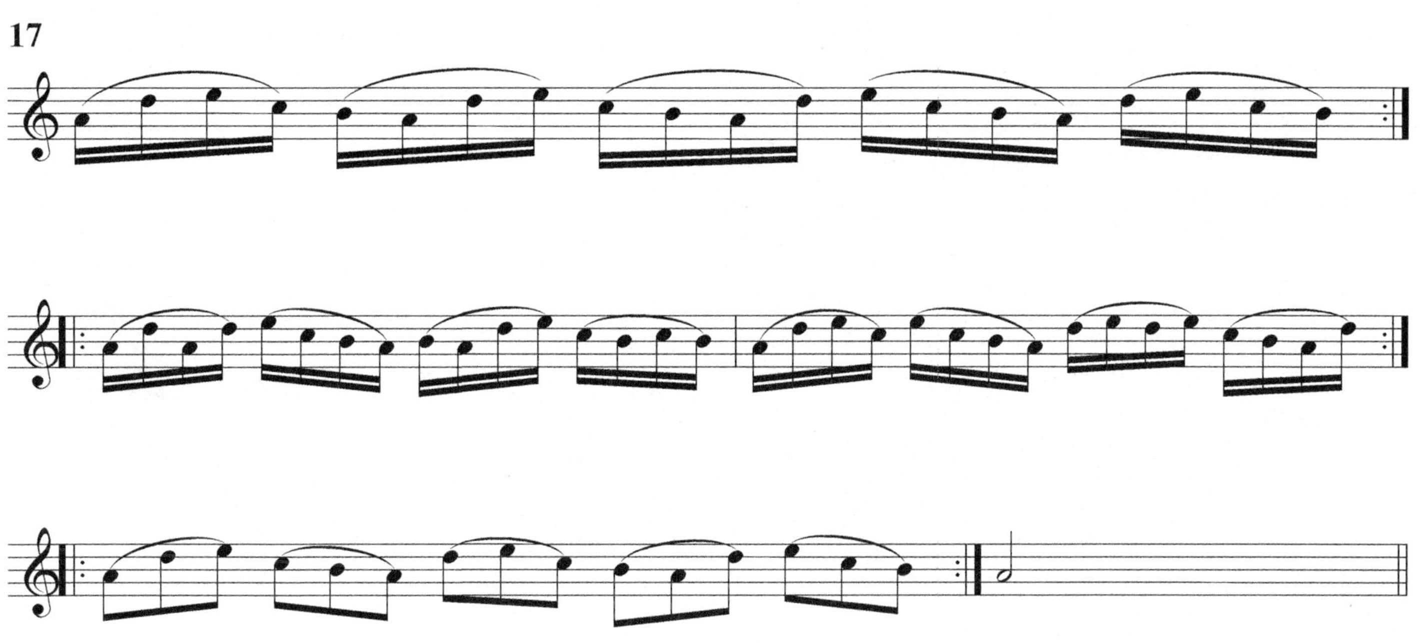

Retain fingers. See line 2. Apply principle throughout.

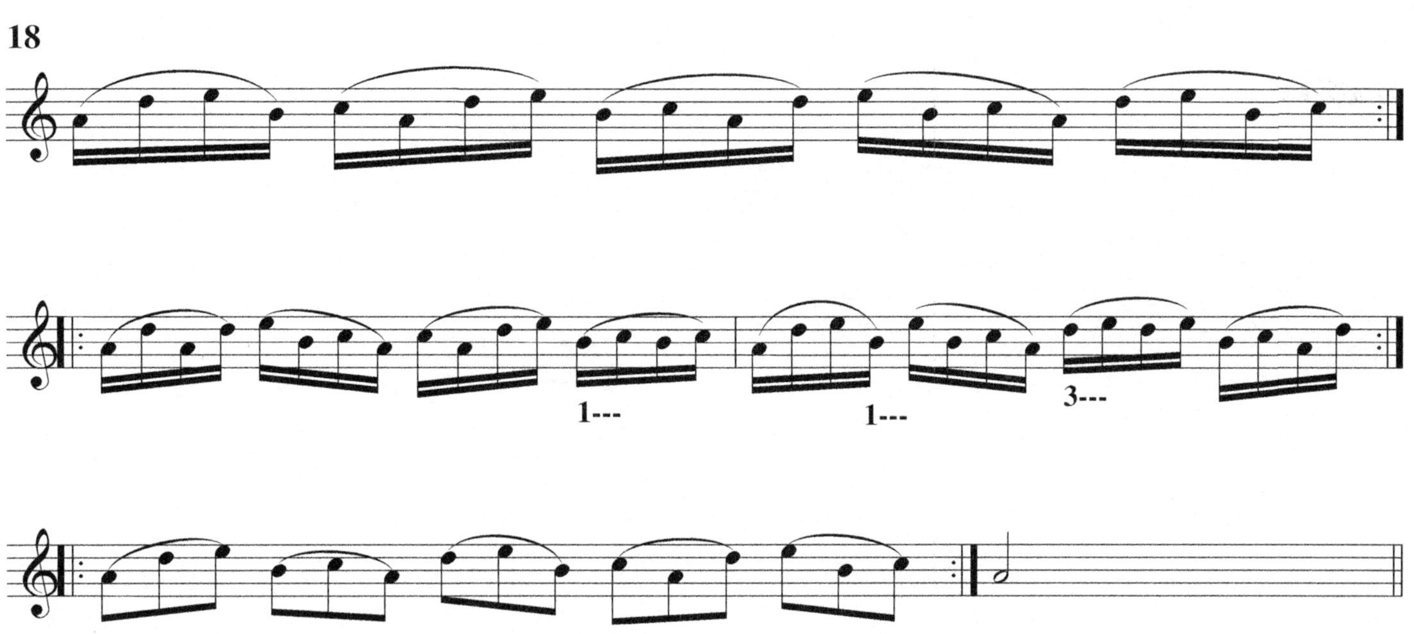

19

20

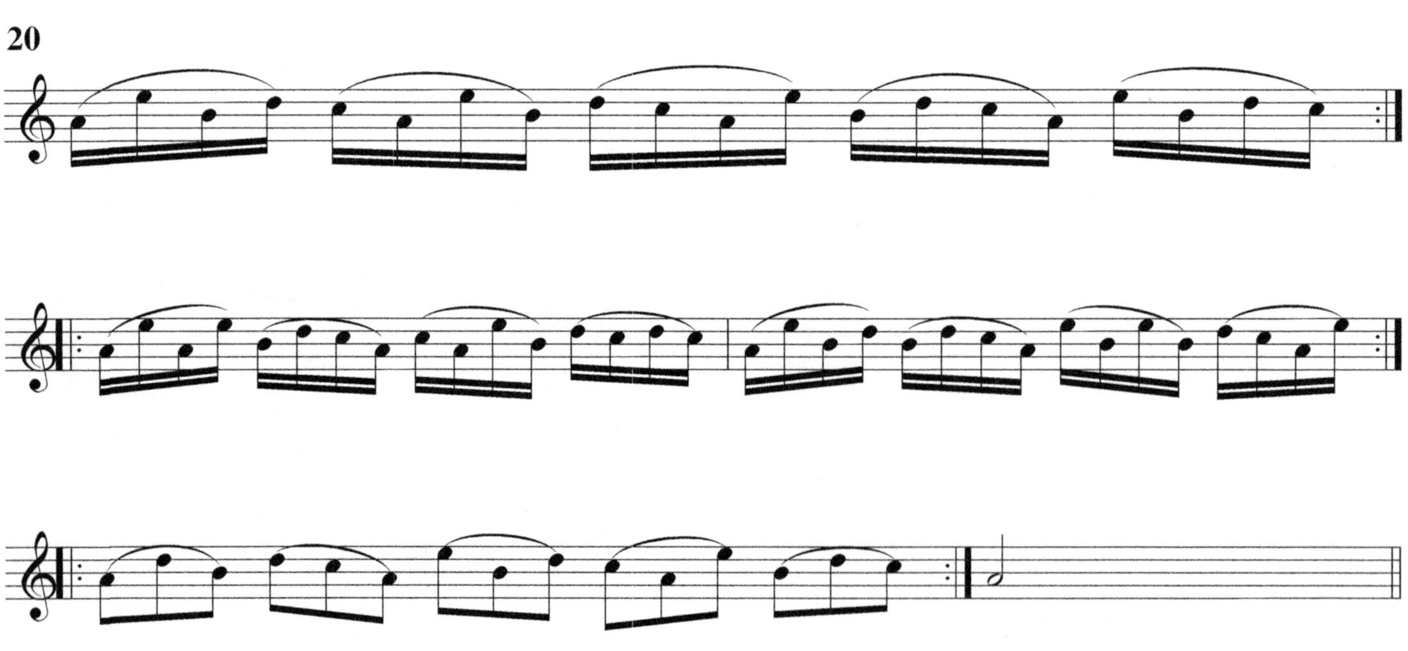

Focus energy in left fingers...quiet hand.

21

Slap high fourth finger.

22

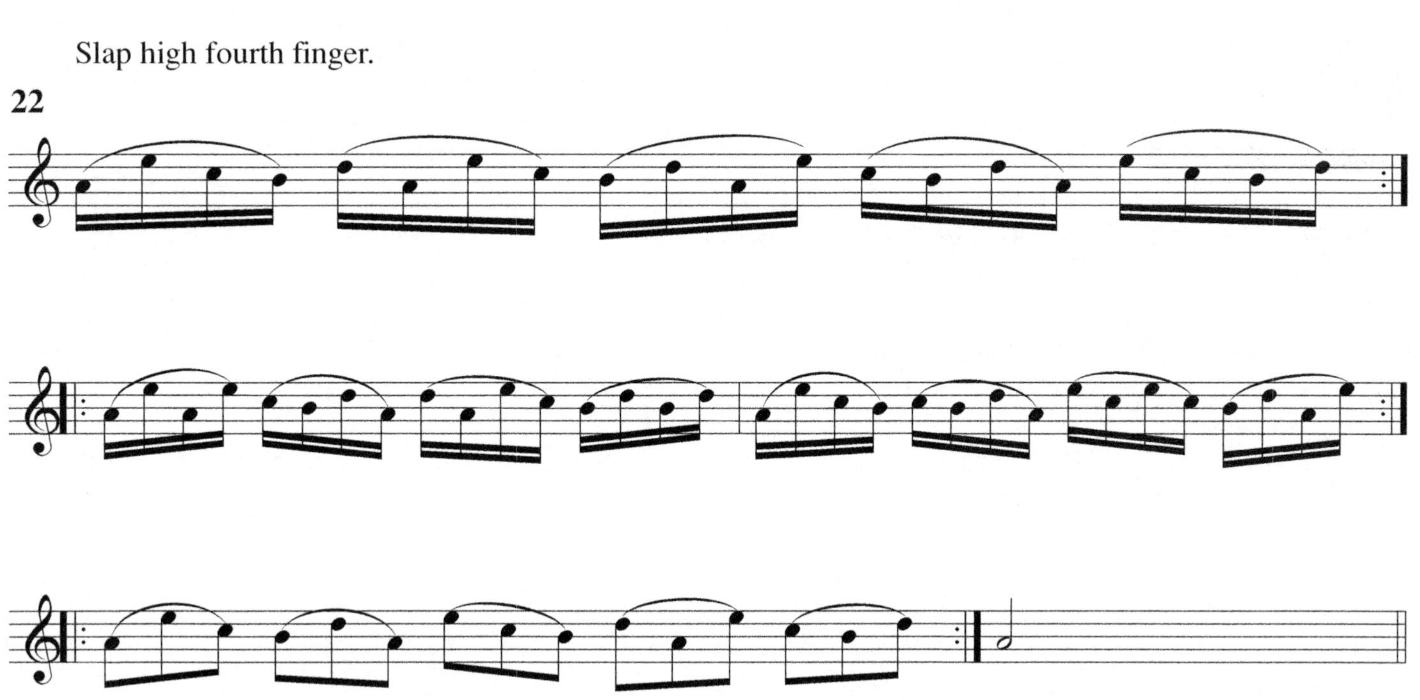

Easy Attitude

23

24

Eventually patterns 25-48 should be practiced in the Major key signatures of F,
G, A, B flat, whole tones and in semi-tones. Triplets are for augmented seconds.

25

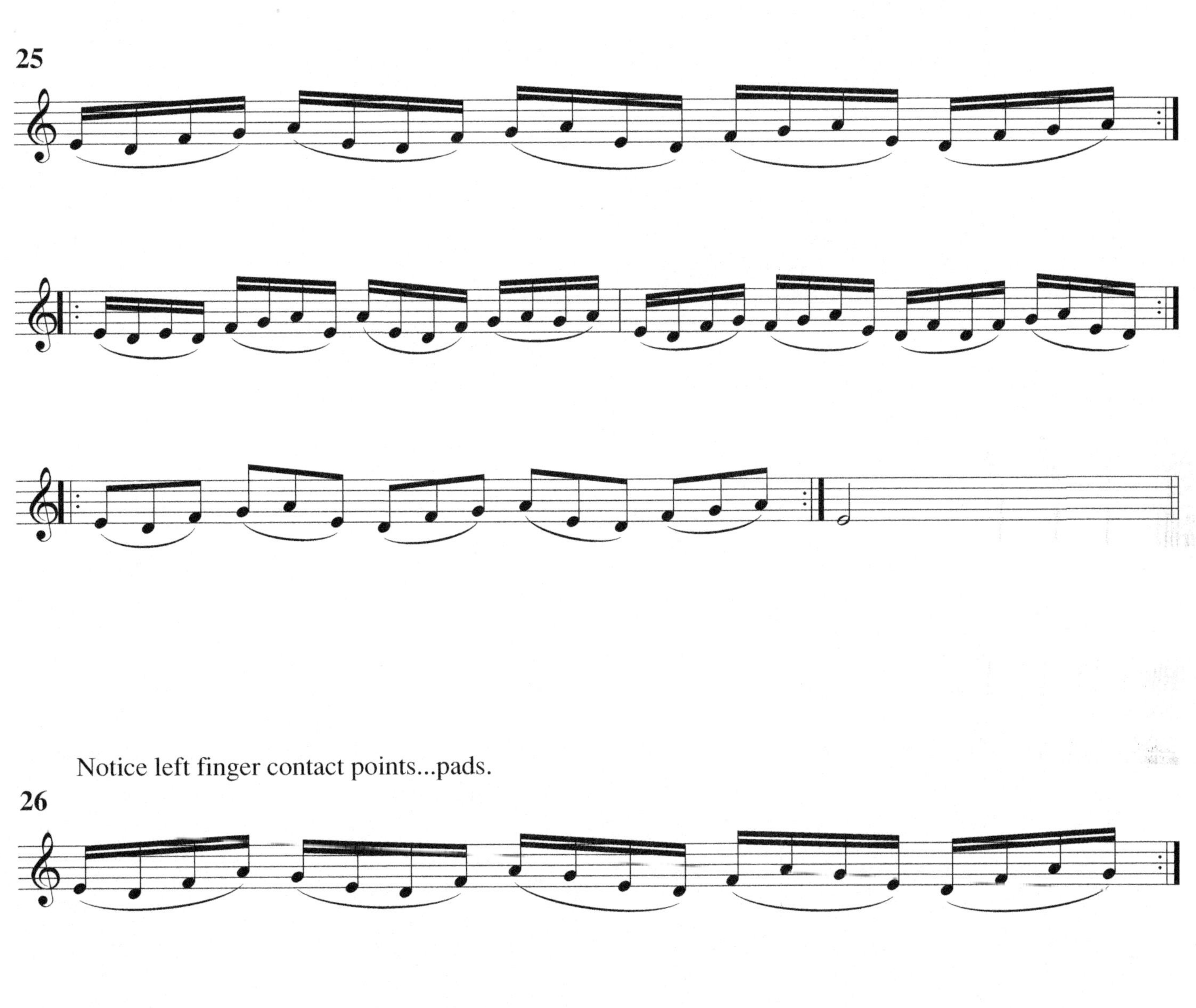

Notice left finger contact points...pads.

26

Left finger contact should be centered or a little to left side of string.

27

28

29

Always take repeats

30

Check left thumb placement

33

Keep idle fingers over string being played

34

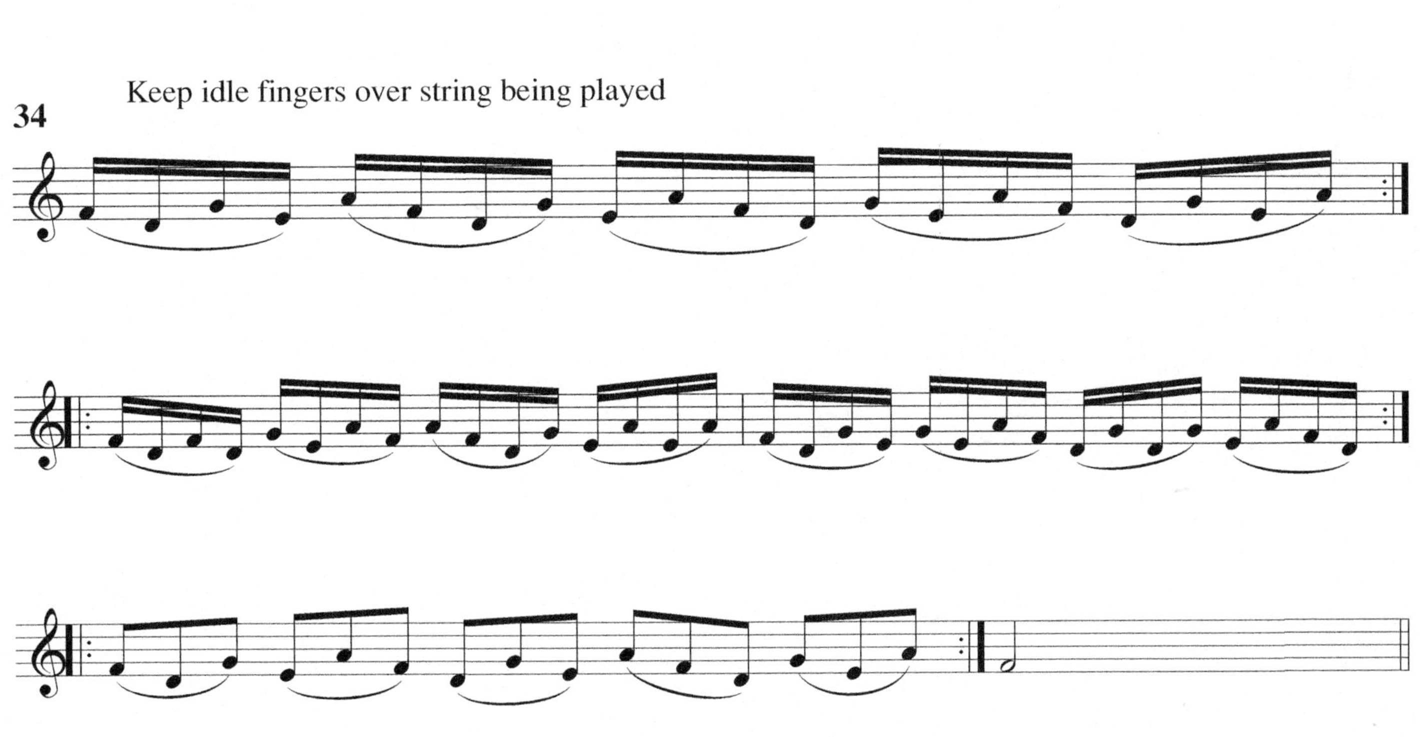

35

36

Easy Attitude

39

40

41

42

44

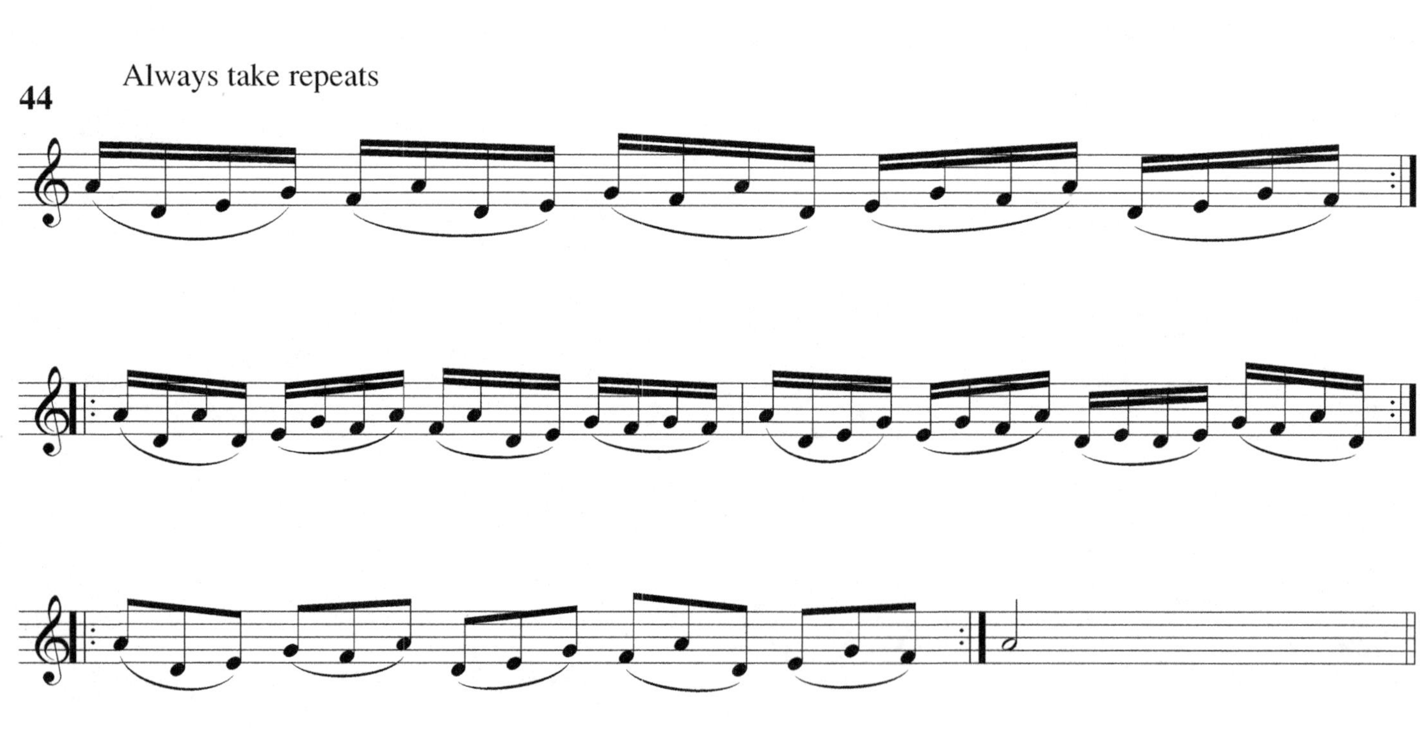

Keep idle fingers over string being played

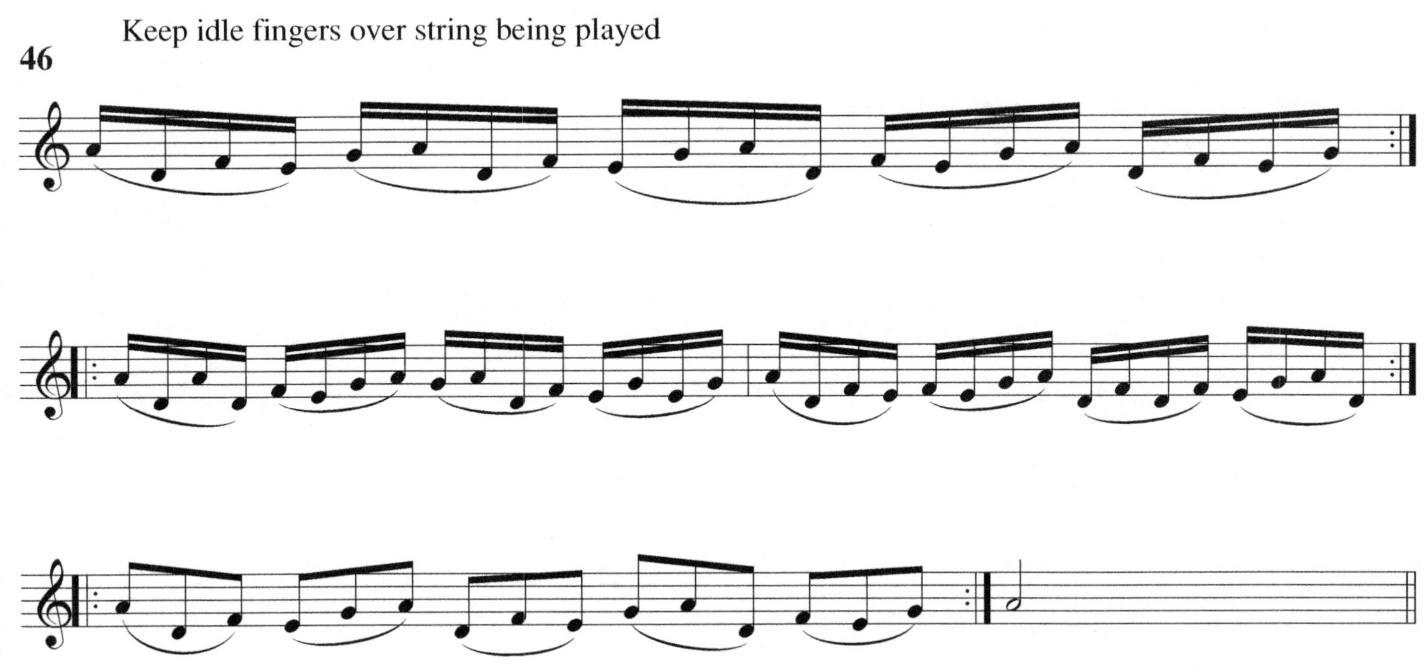

47

48

Eventually studies 49-72 should be practiced in the Major key signatures of B flat, C, D, E flat, whole tones, and half steps. Triplets are for augmented seconds.

49

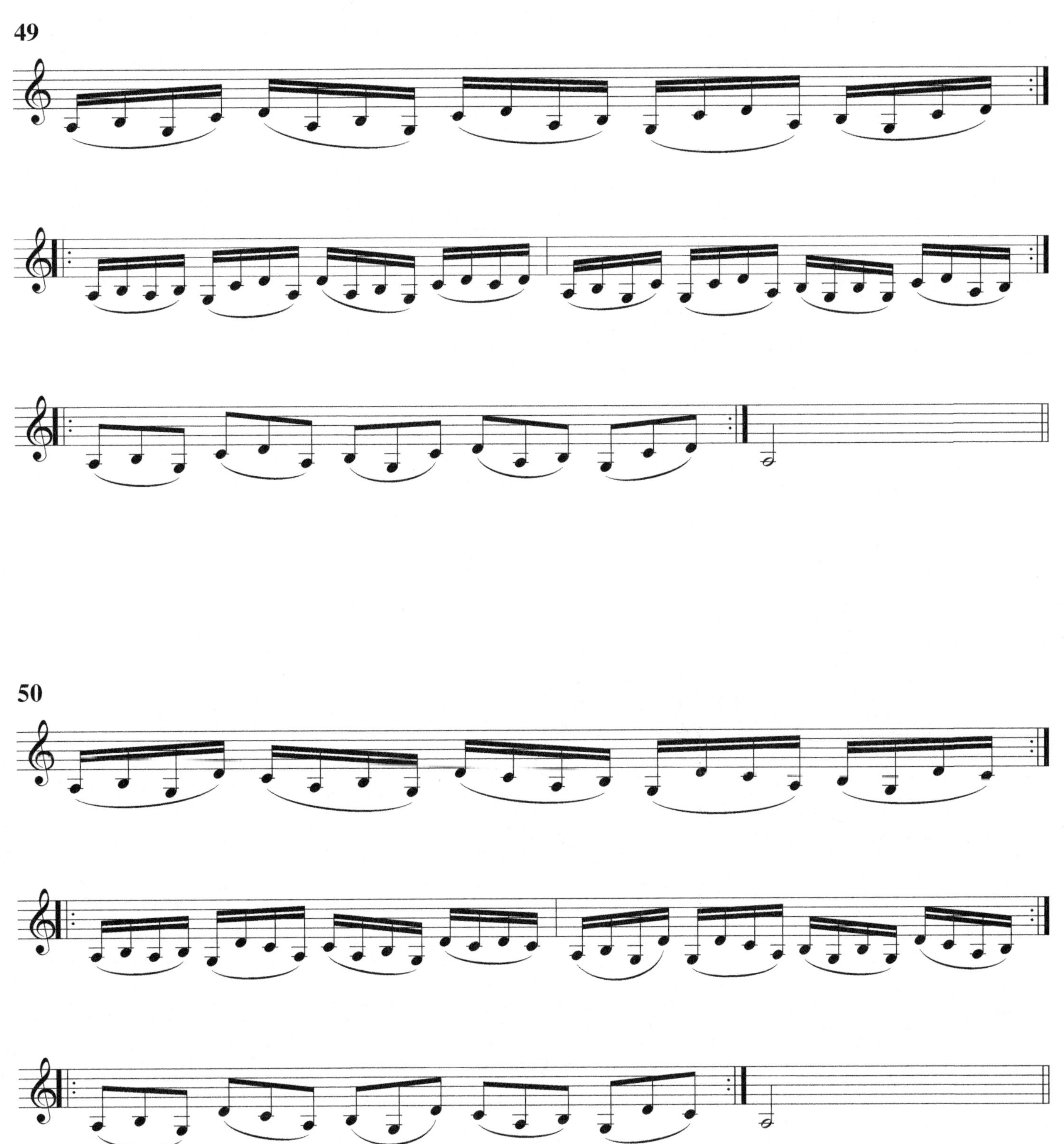

50

51

Always take repeats

52

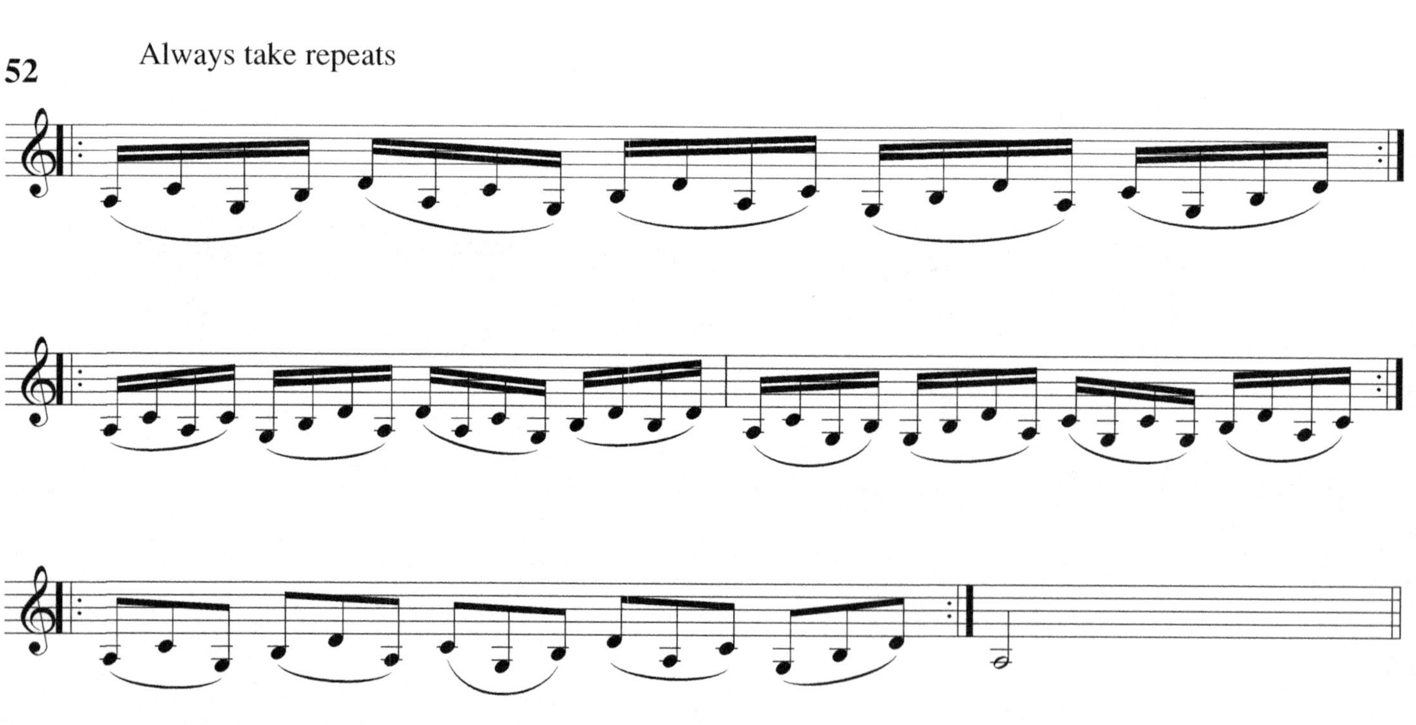

53

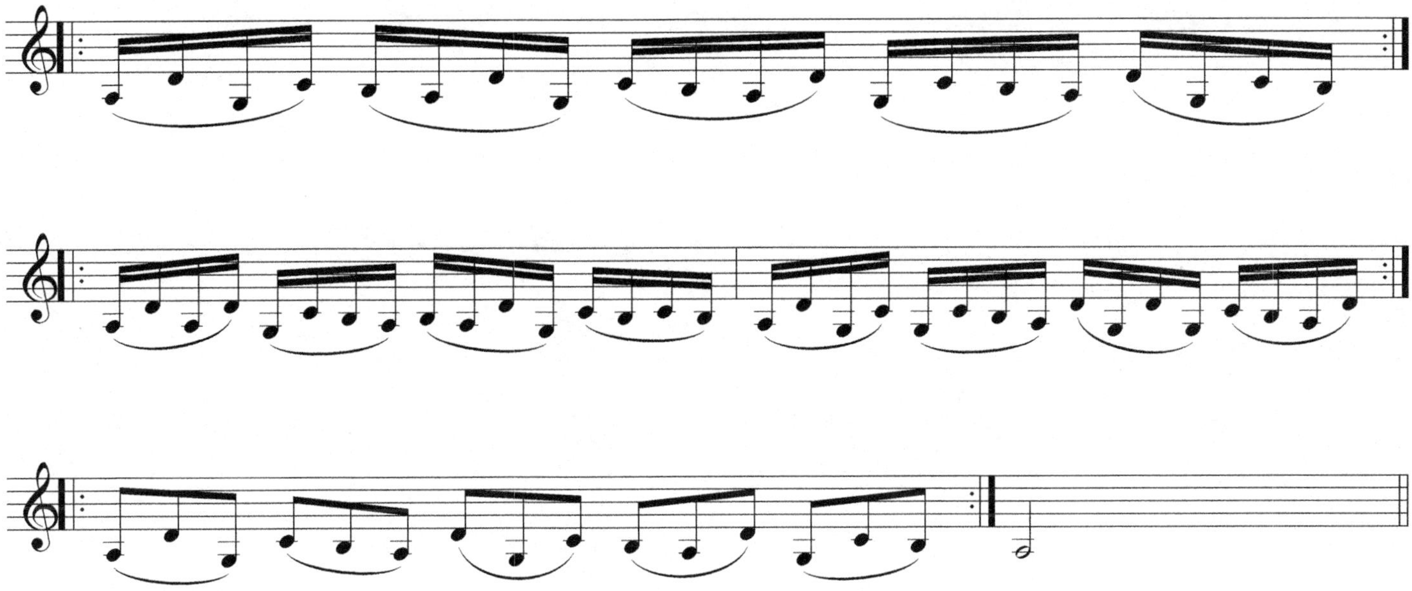

54

55

56

57

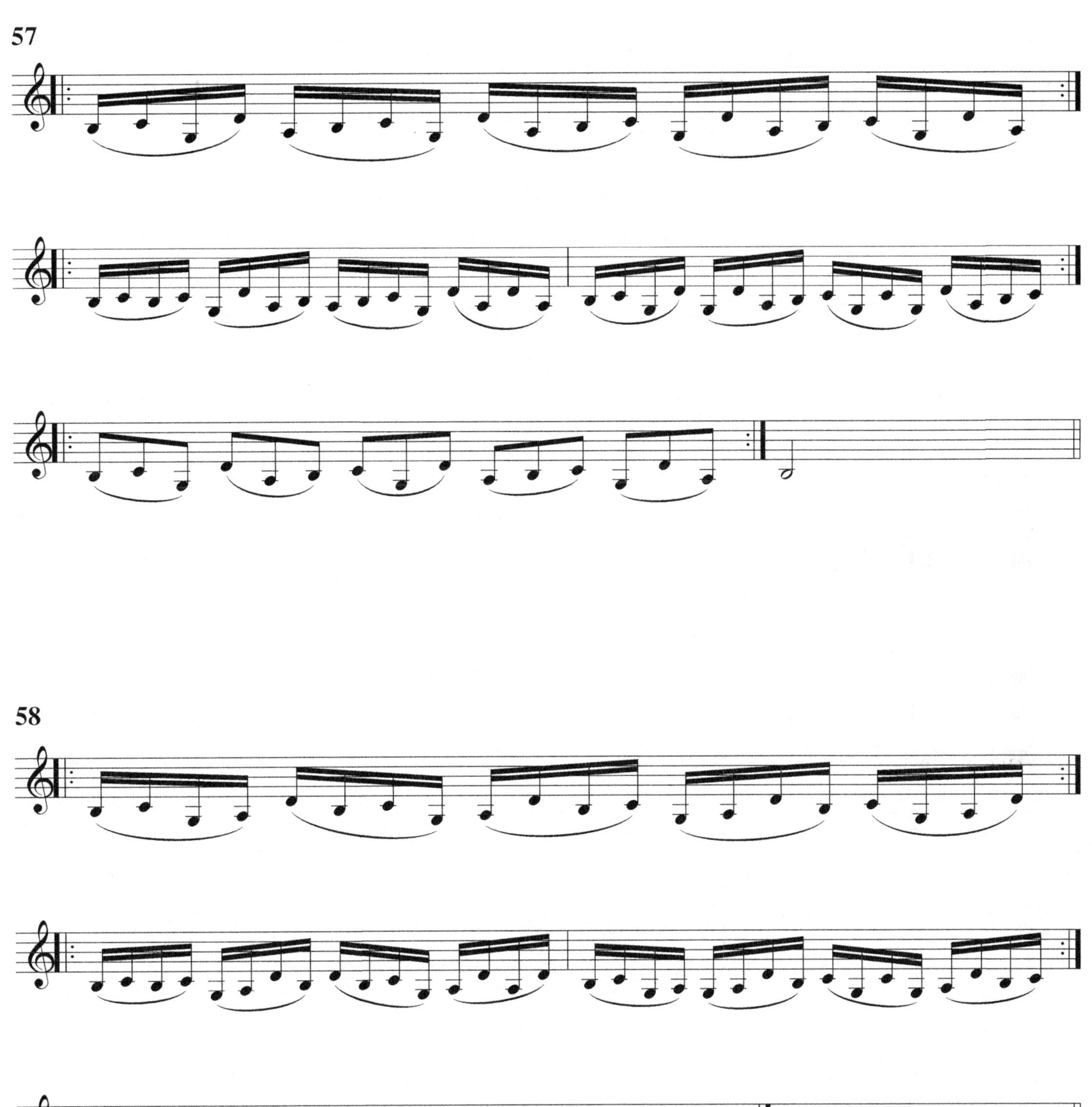

58

Easy Attitude

59

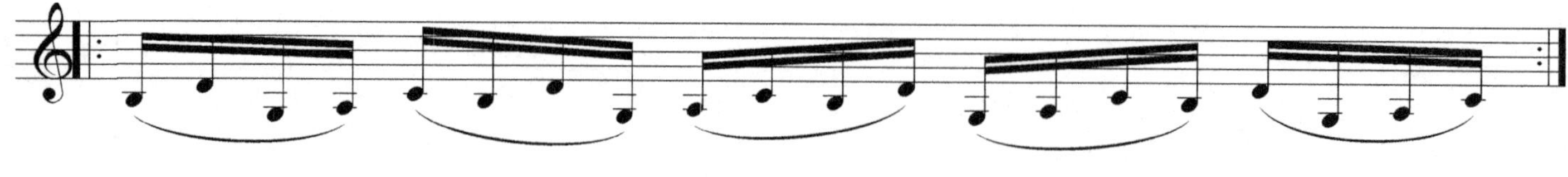

Check left thumb placement

60

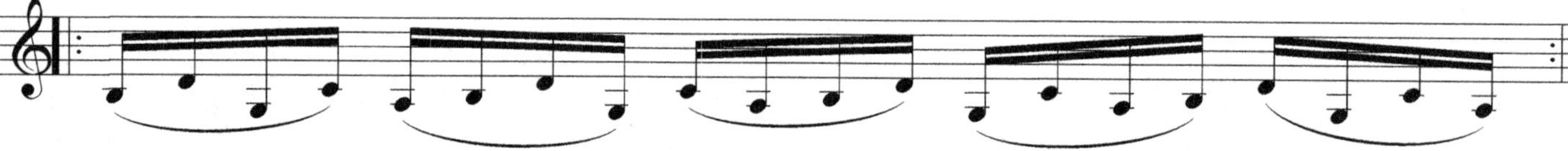

61

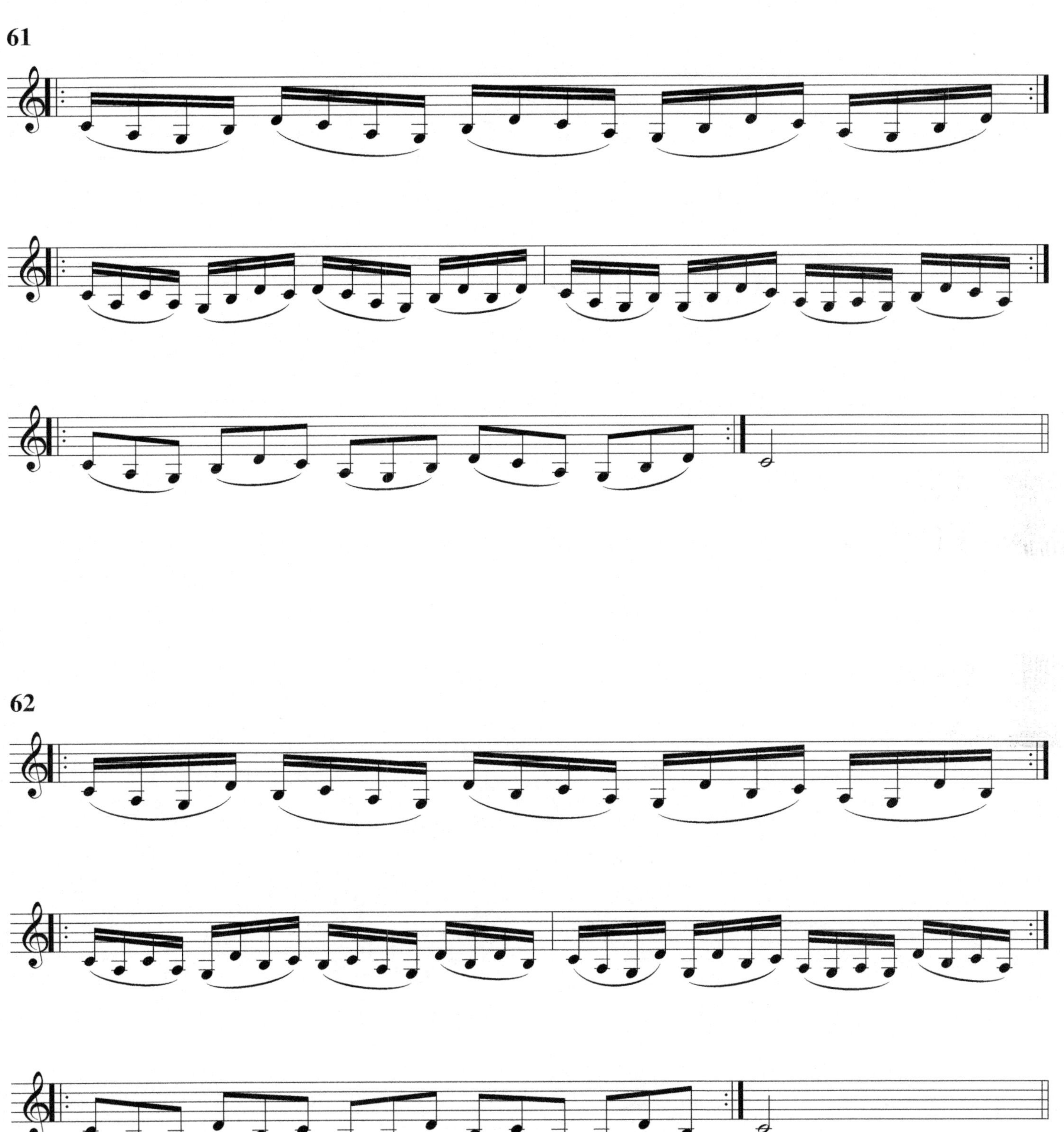

62

63

64

65

Keep idle fingers over string being played

66

67

68

69

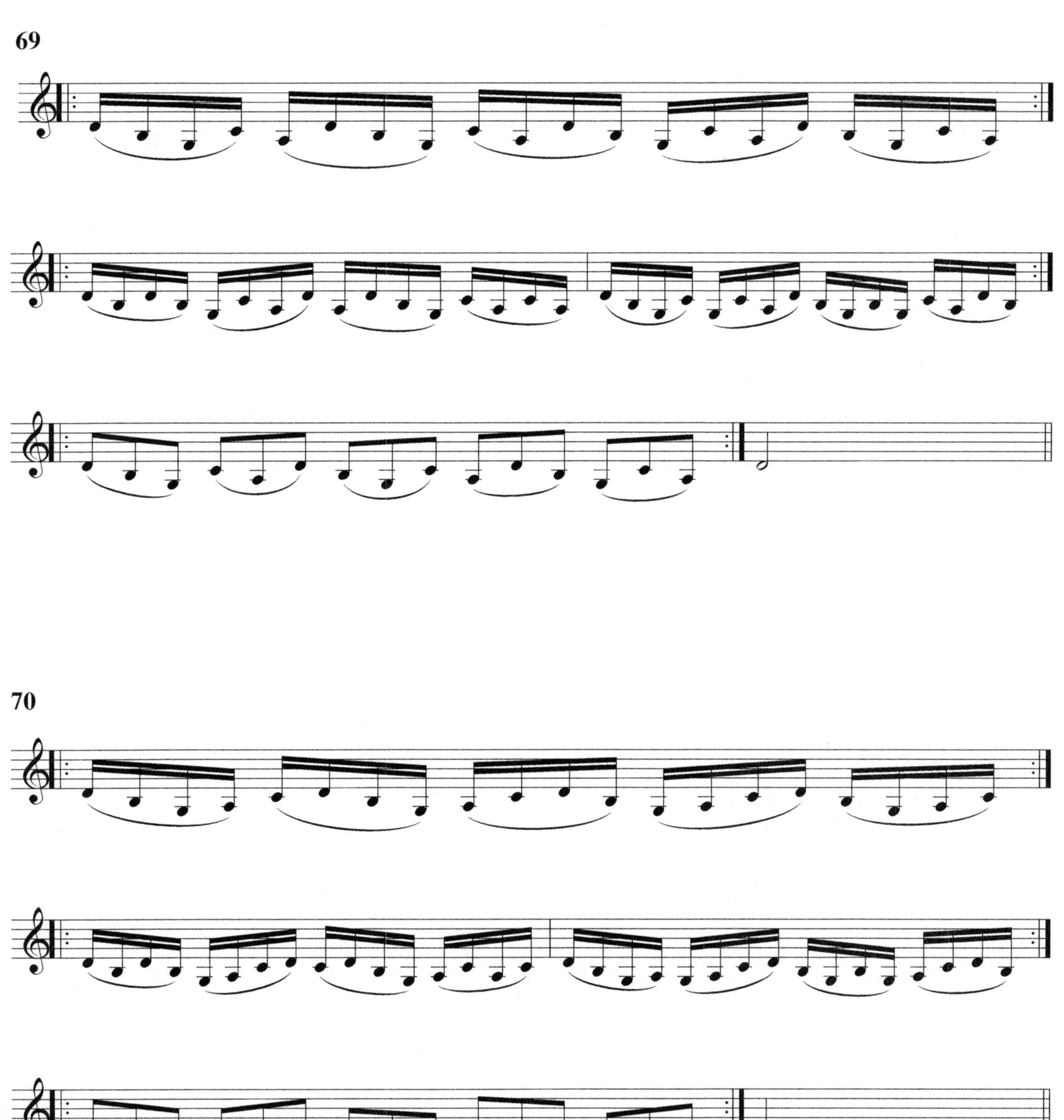

70

71

72

Eventually patterns 73-96 should be practiced in the Major key signatures of G,
A, B, C, whole tones and in semi-tones. Triplets are for augmented seconds.

73

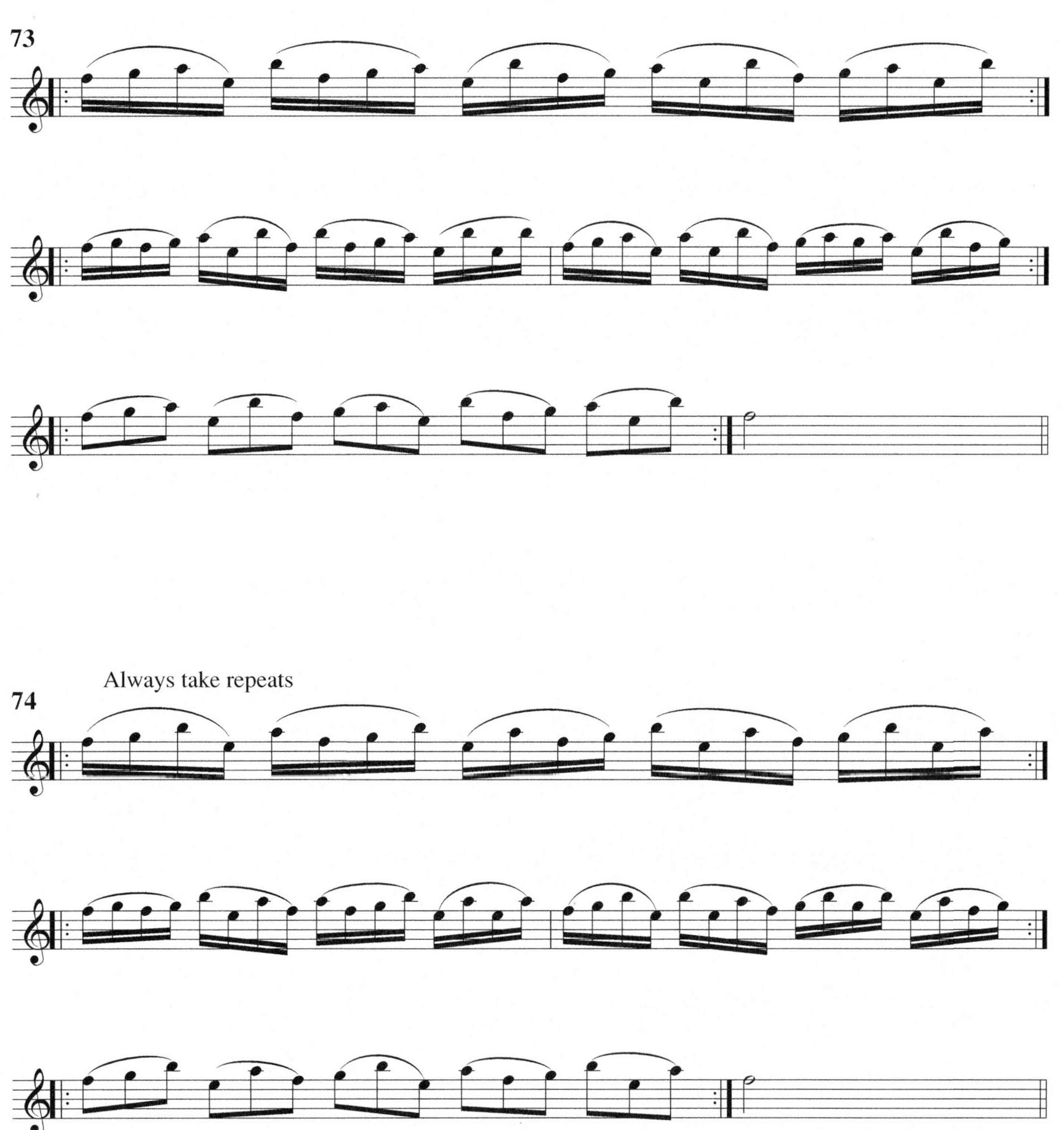

77

78

79

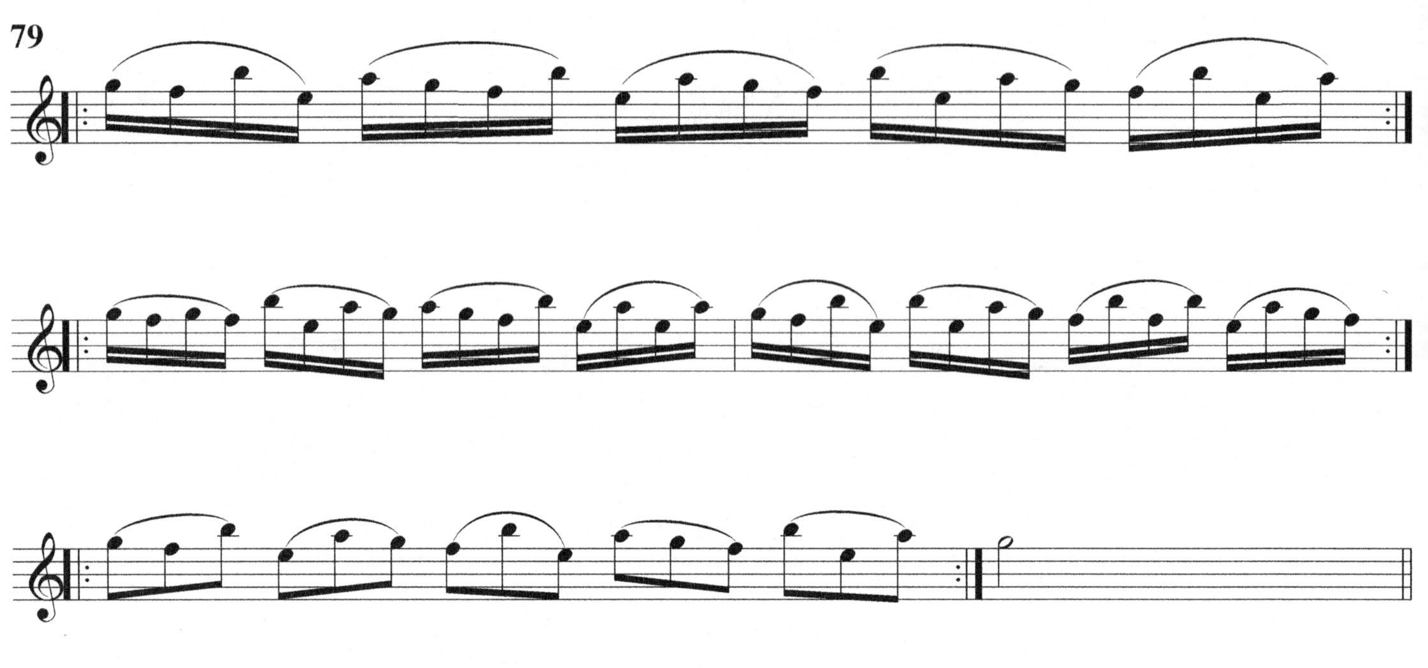

80

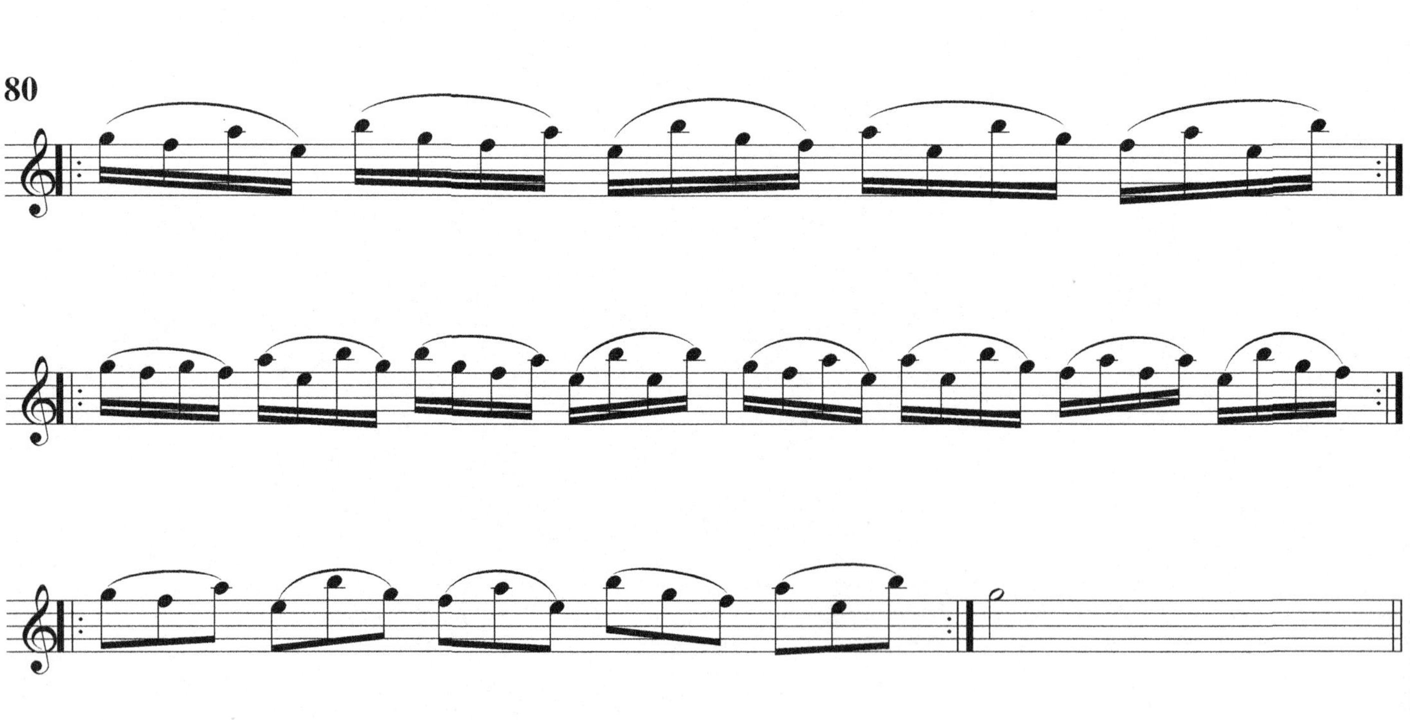

Keep idle fingers over string being played

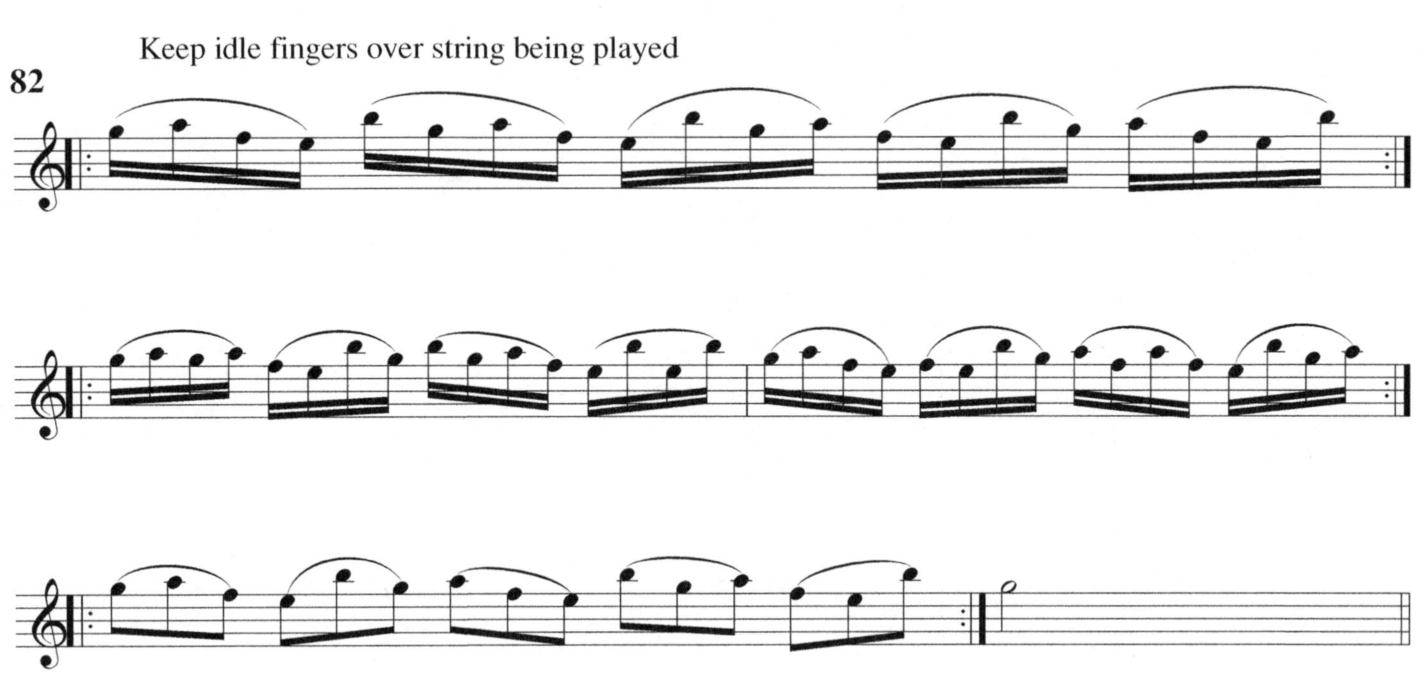

Easy Attitude

83

84

Always take repeats

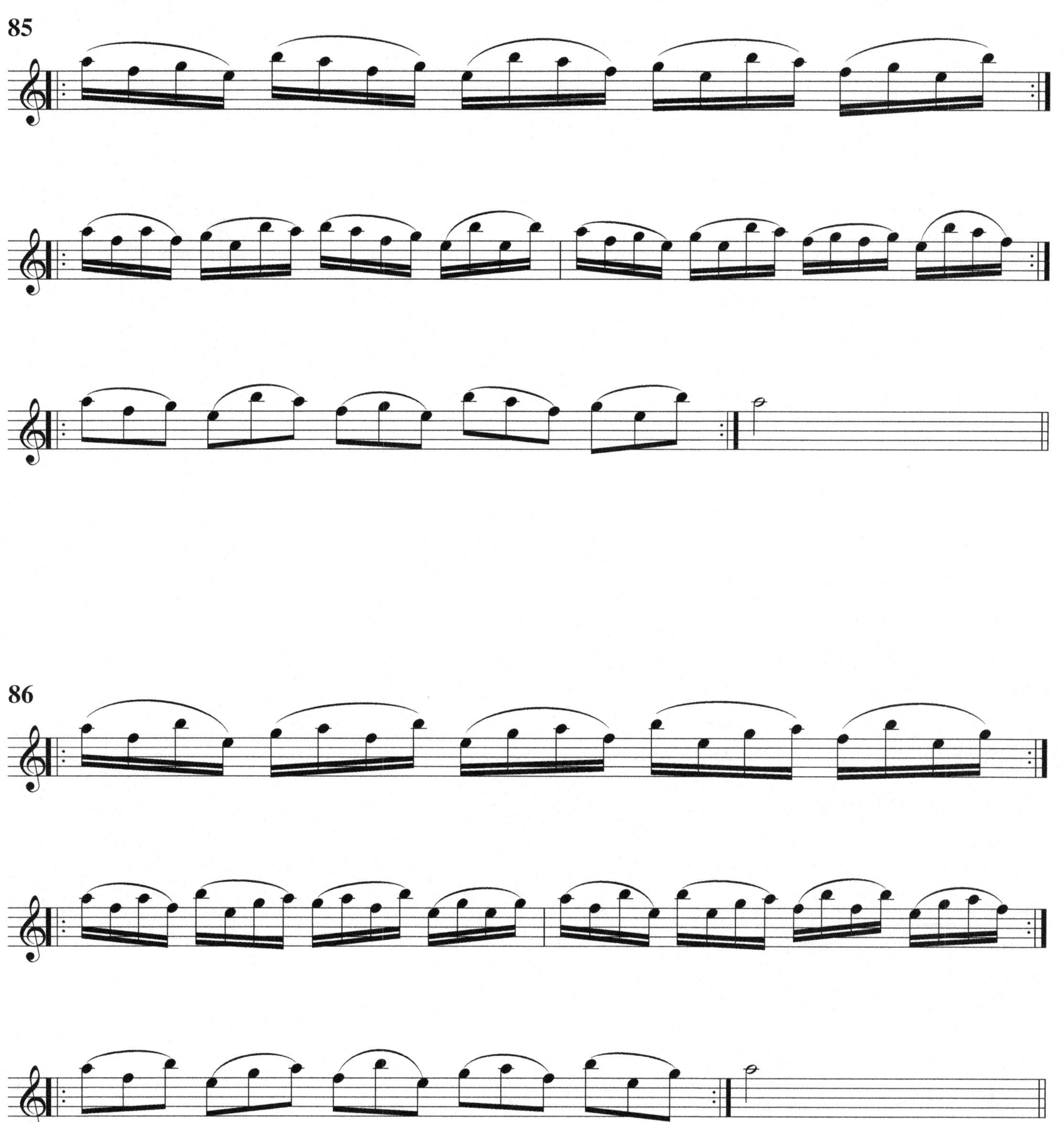
85
86

87

Check left thumb placement

88

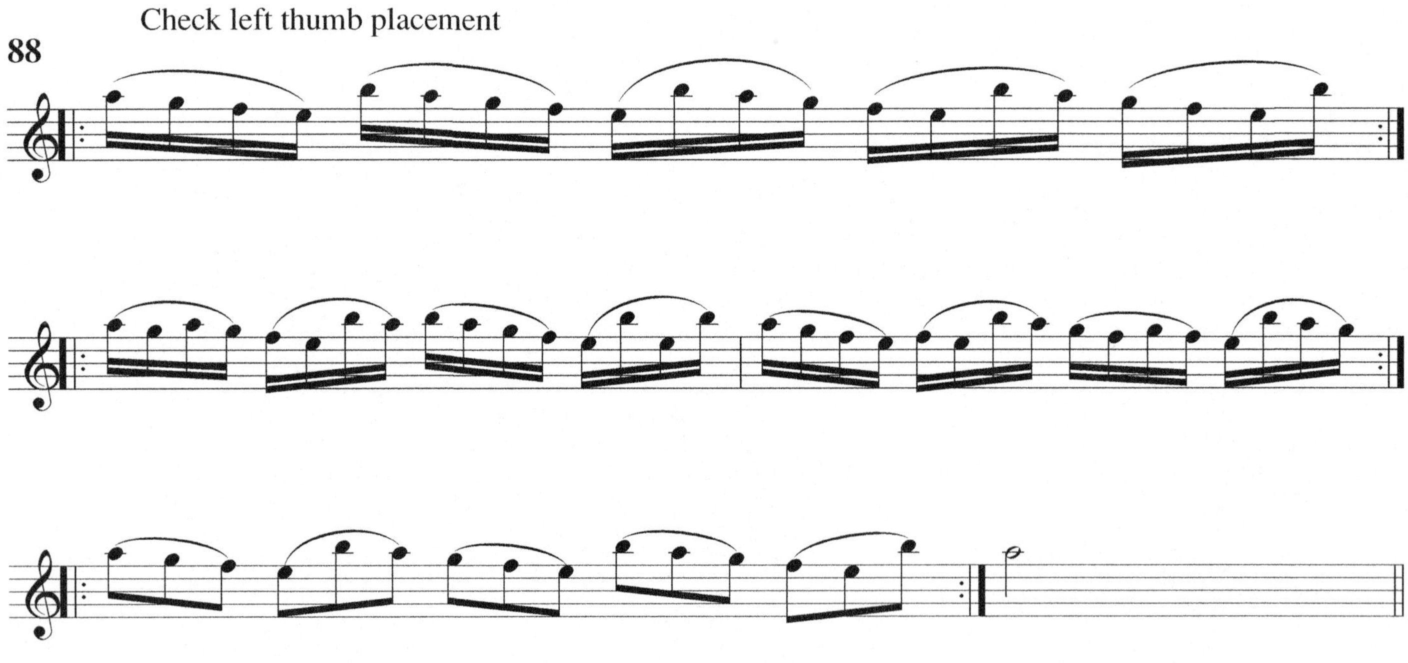

89

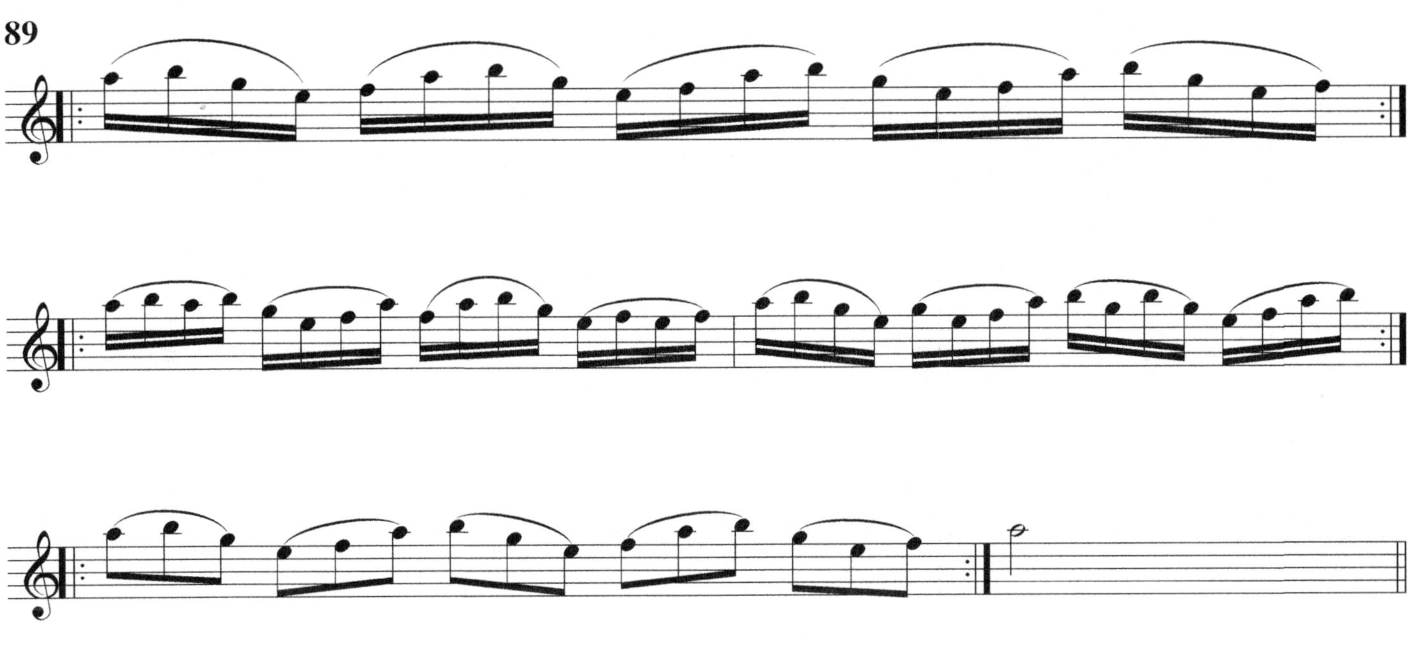

Focus energy in left fingers

90

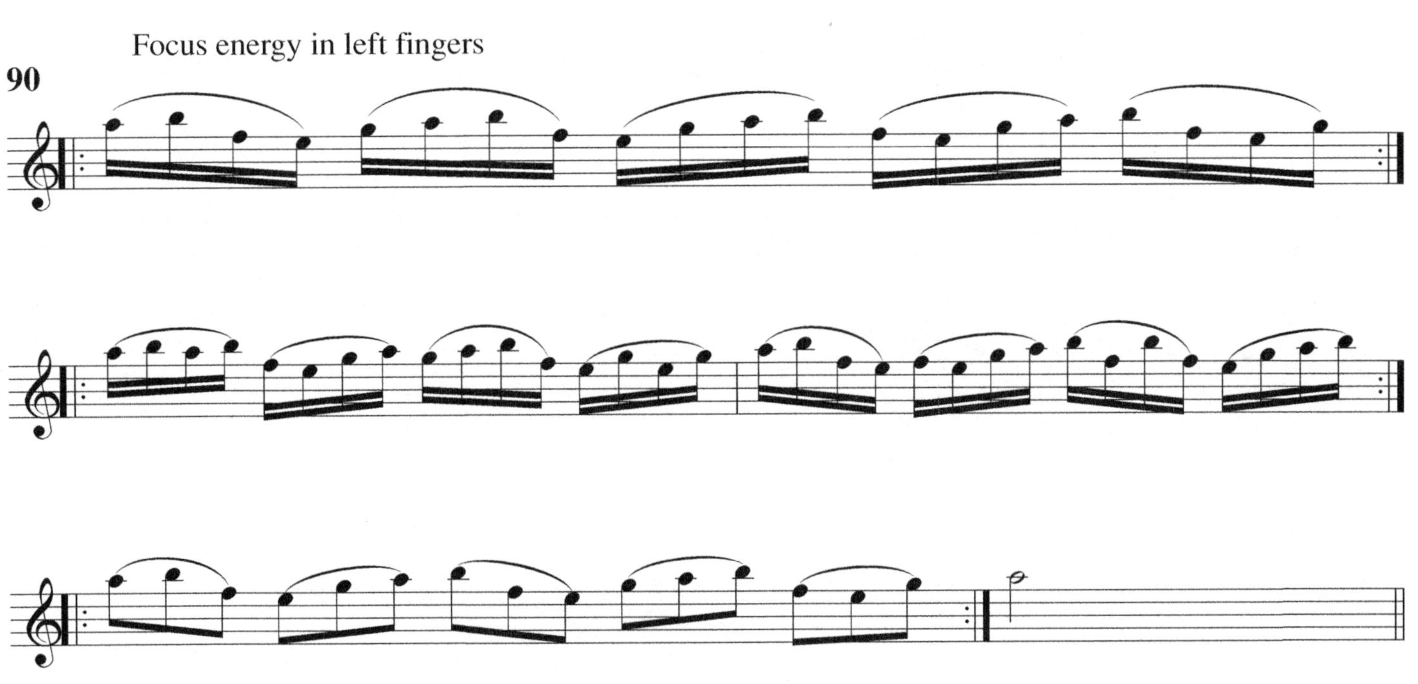

91

92

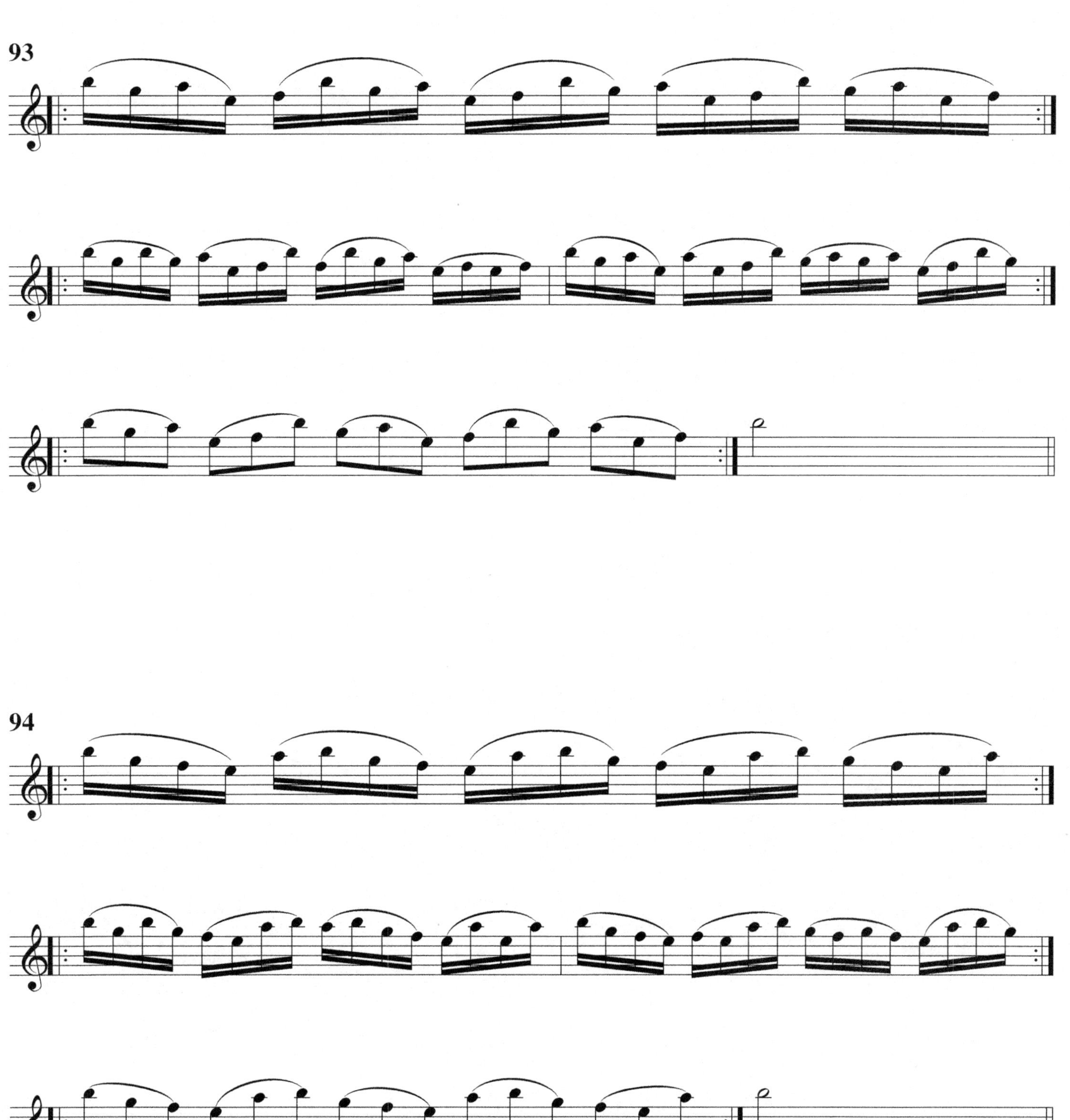

95

96

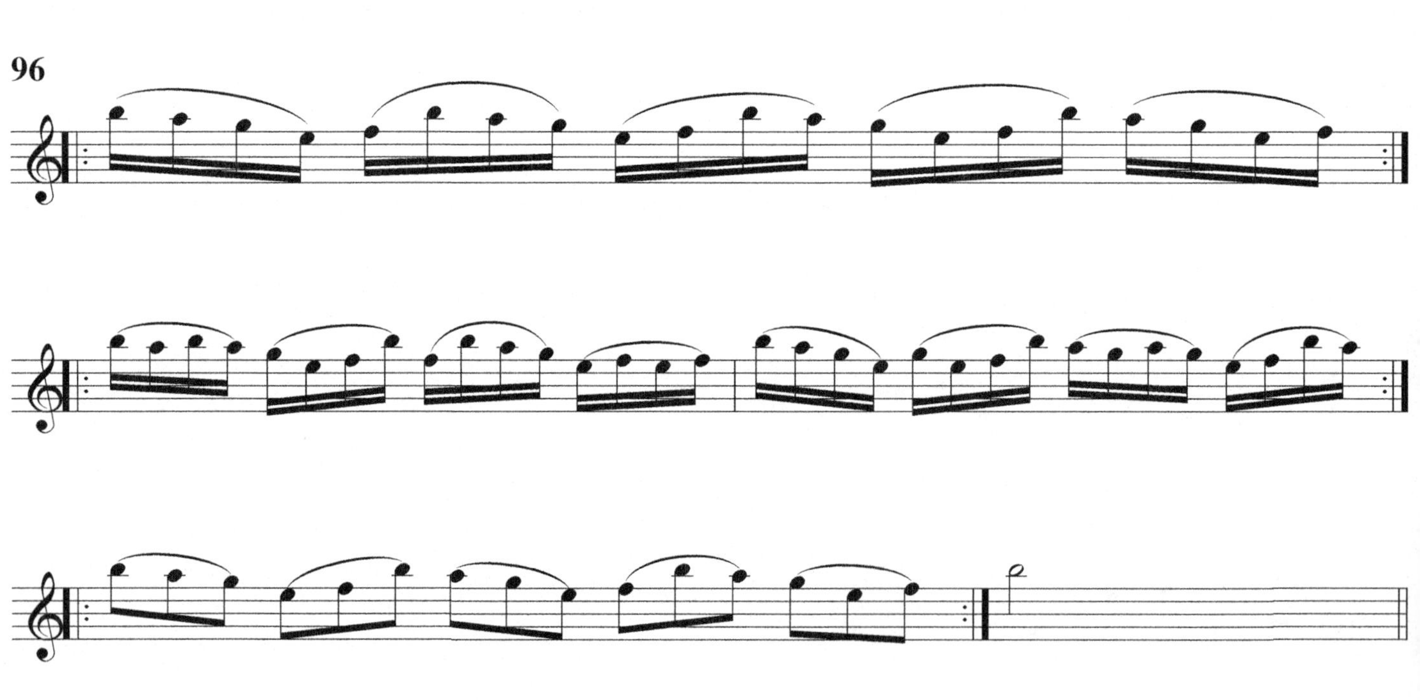

Eventually patterns 97-120 should be practiced in the Major key signatures of C,
D, E, F, whole tones and in semi-tones. Triplets are for augmented seconds.

97

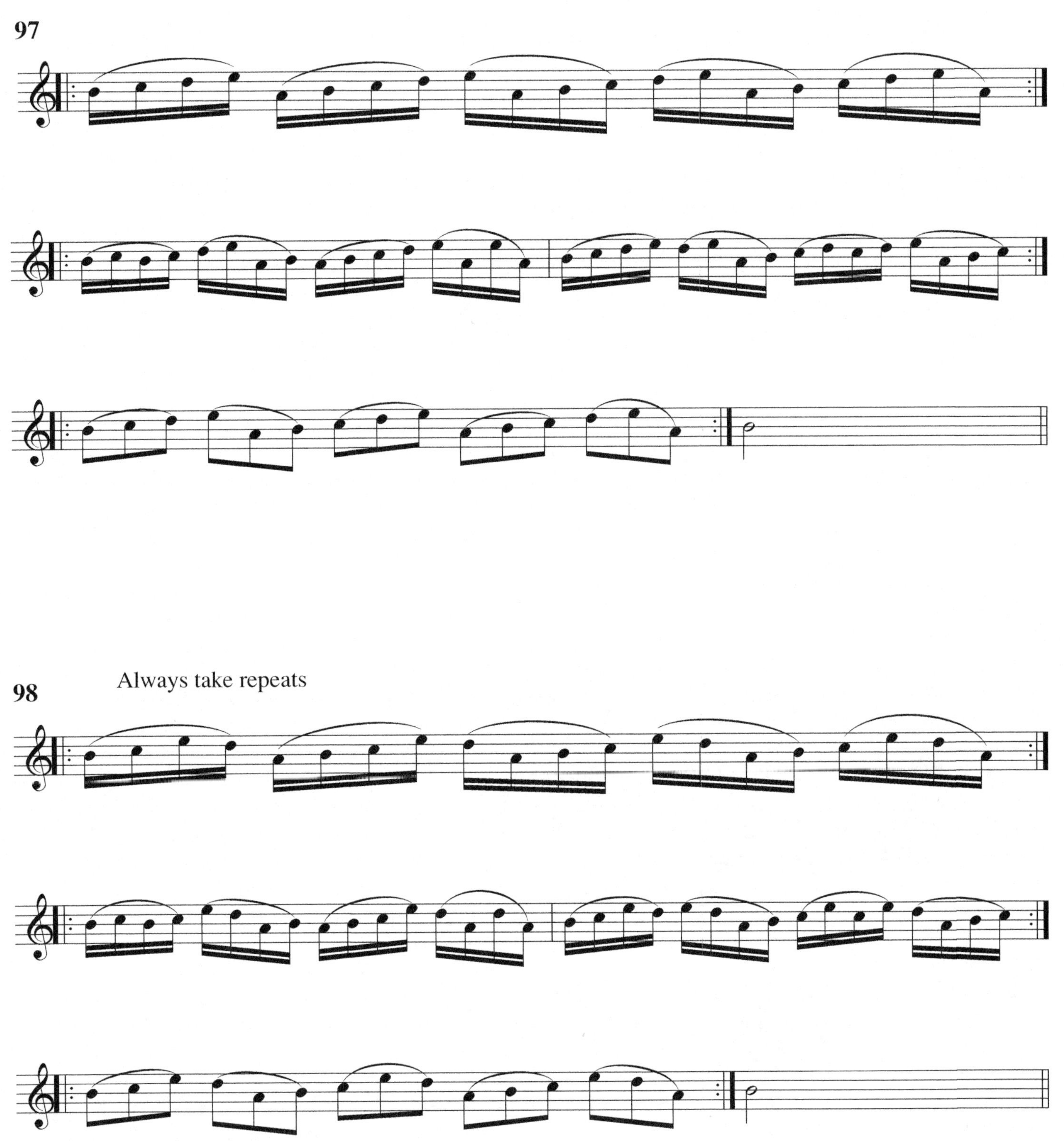

98

99

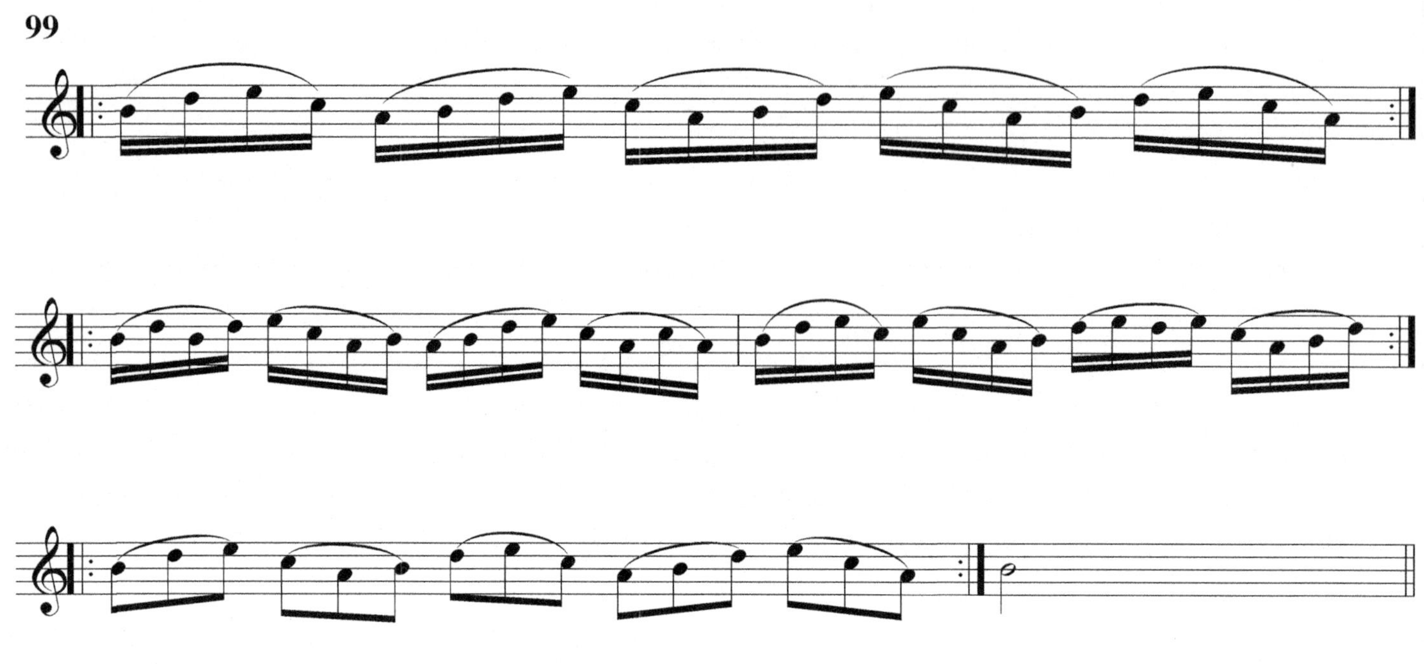

100

Focus energy in left fingers

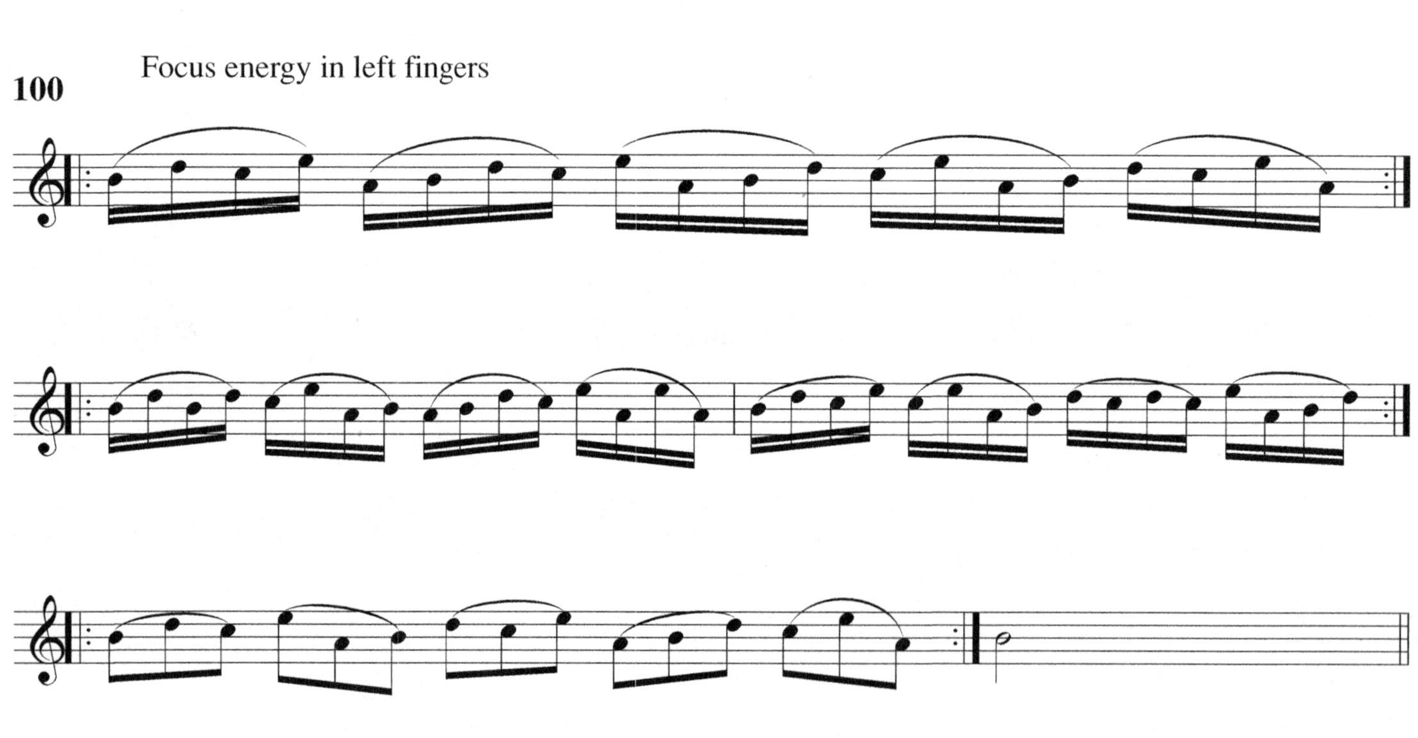

101
102

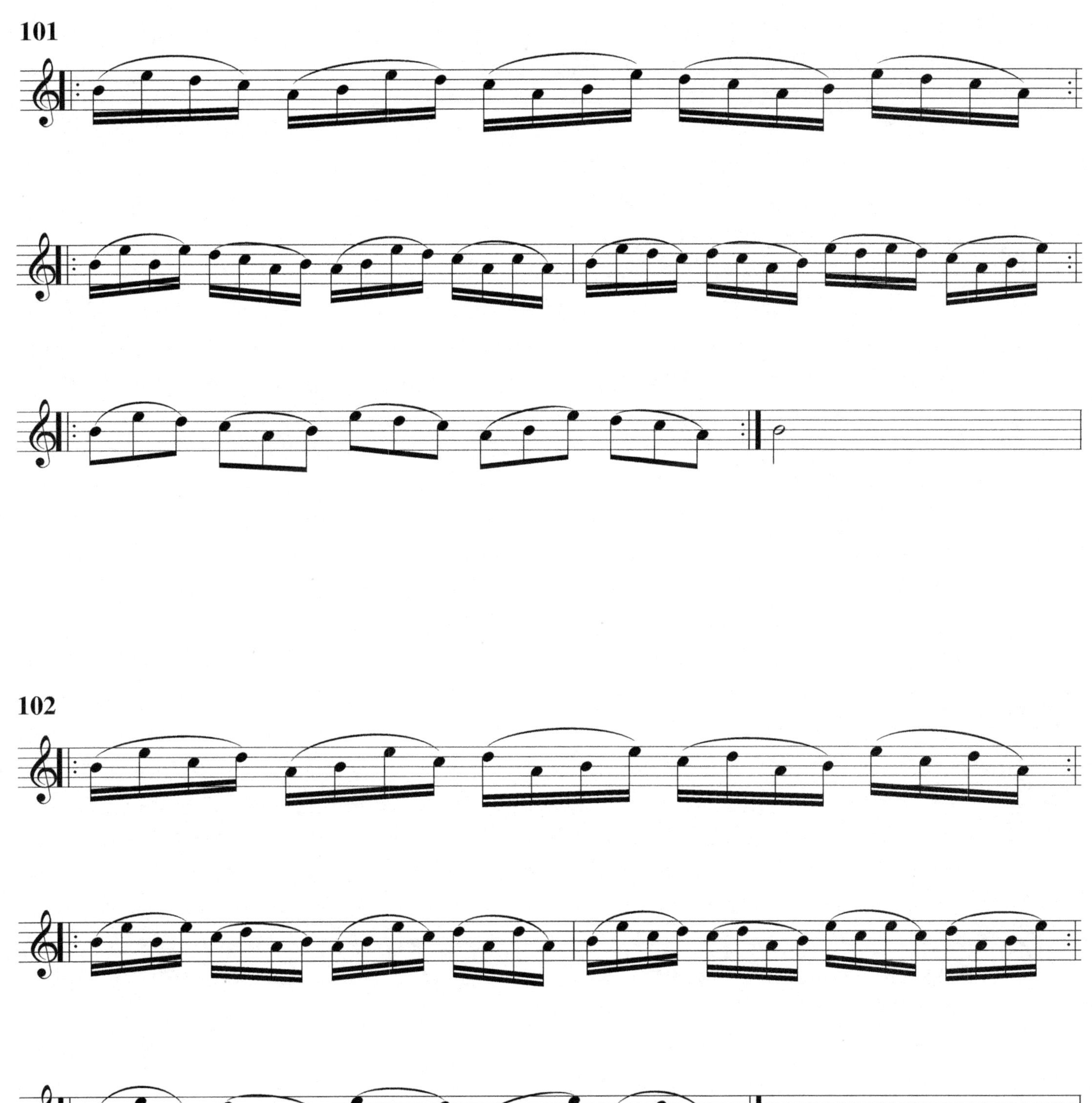

103

104

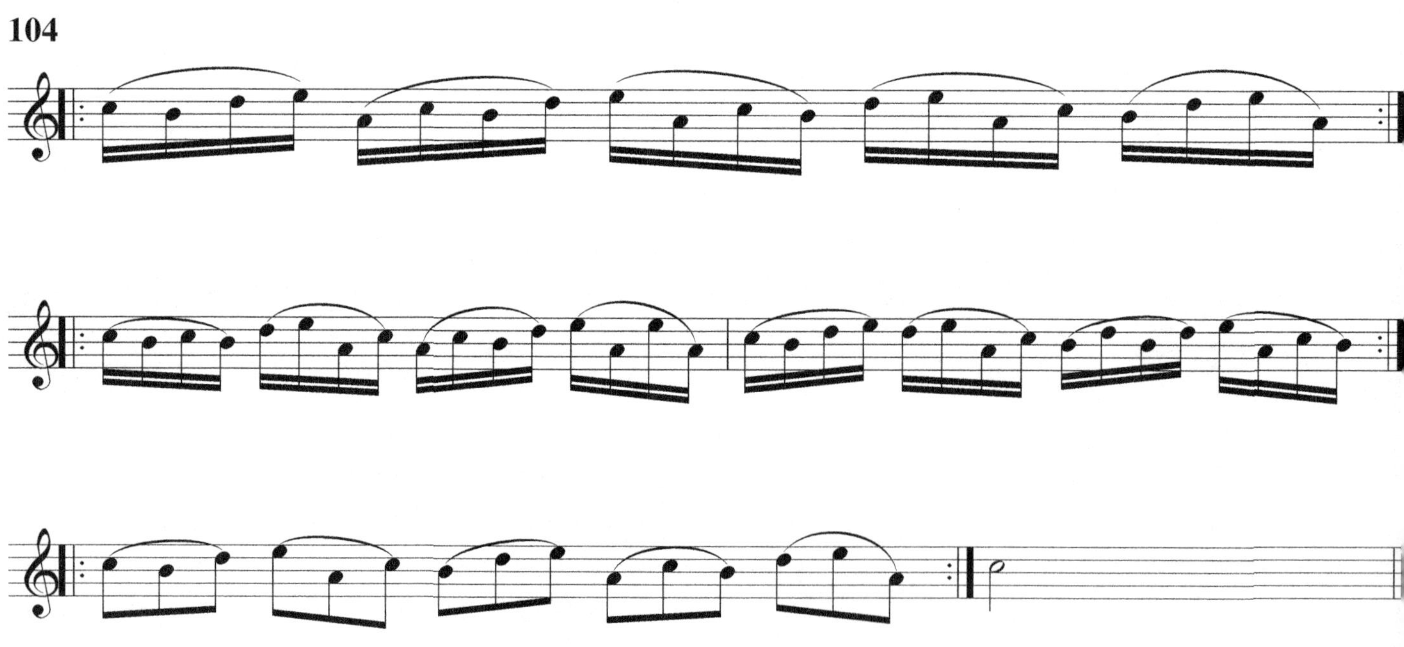

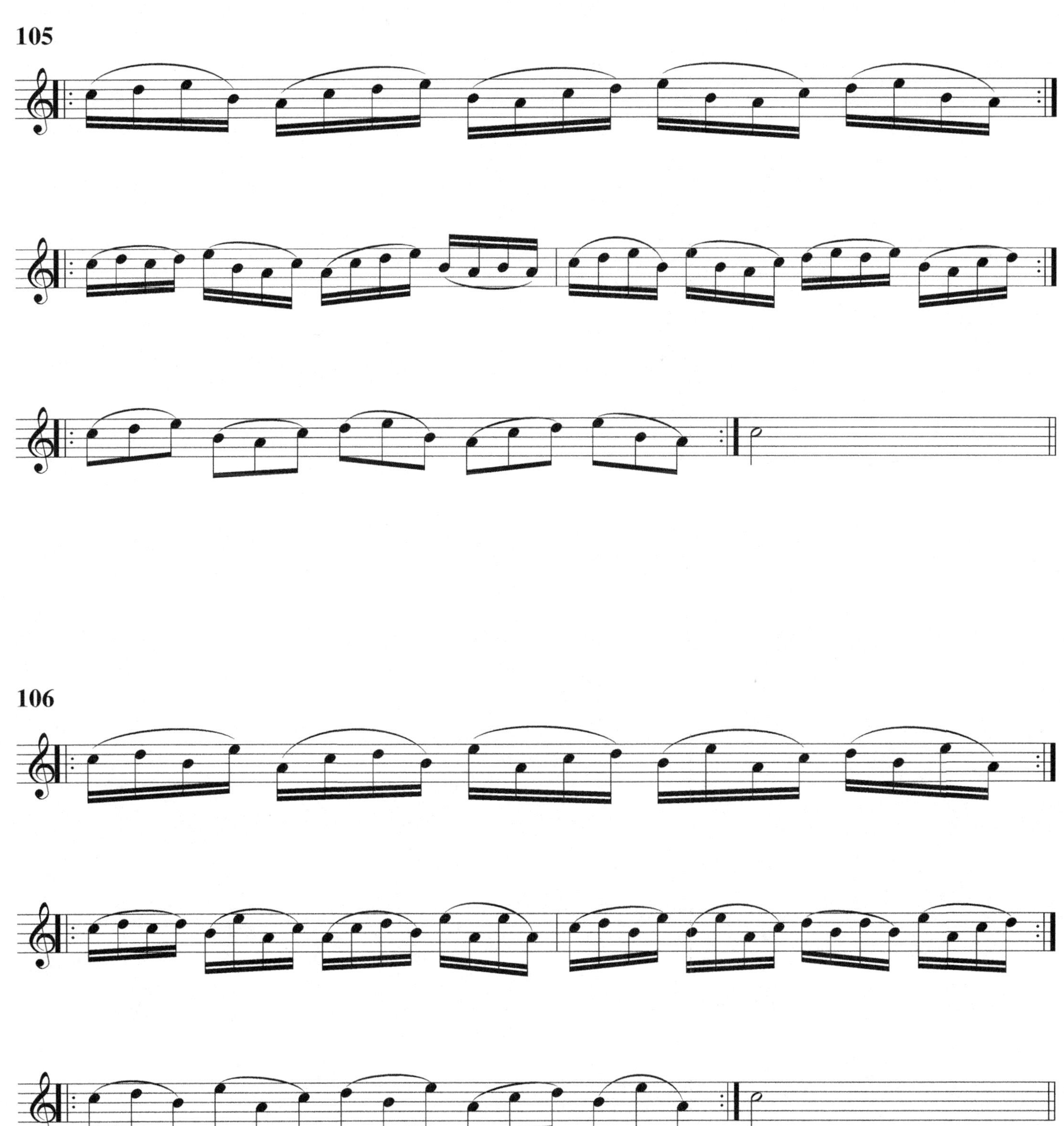

107

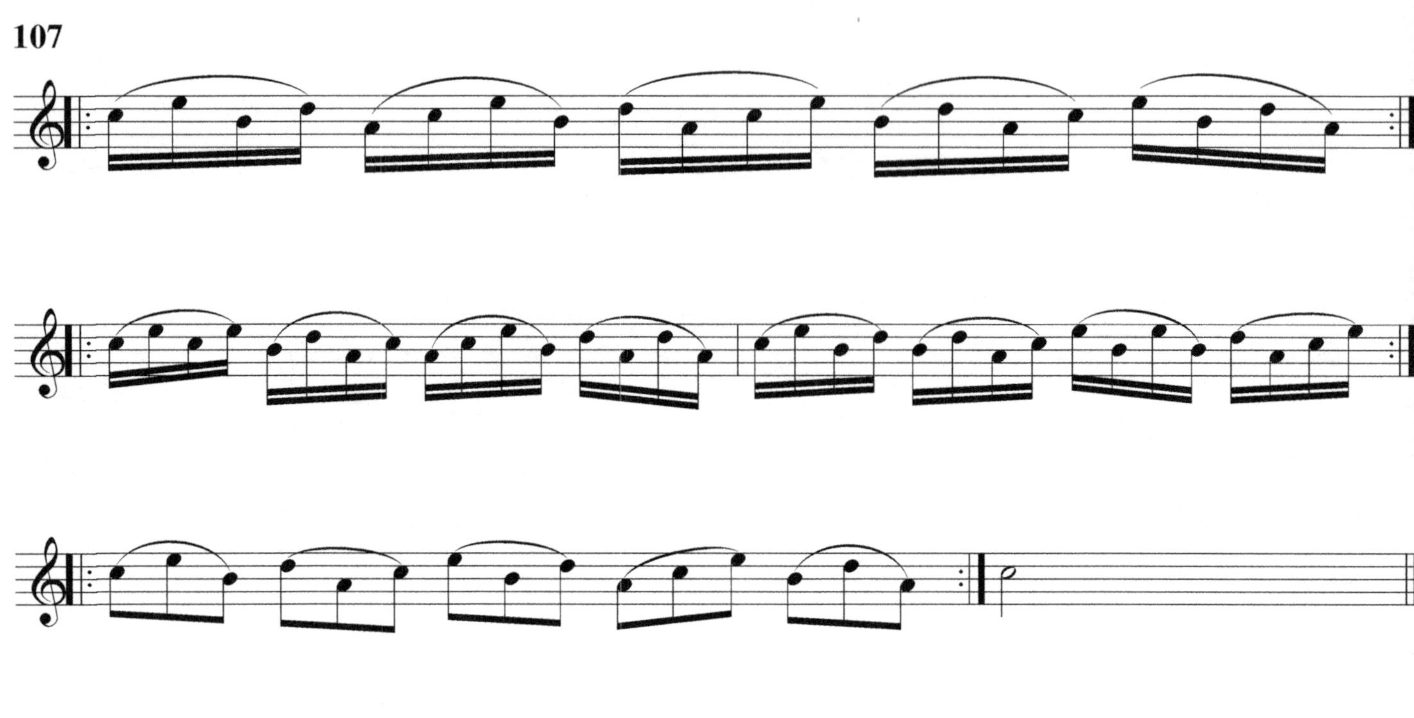

108

109
110

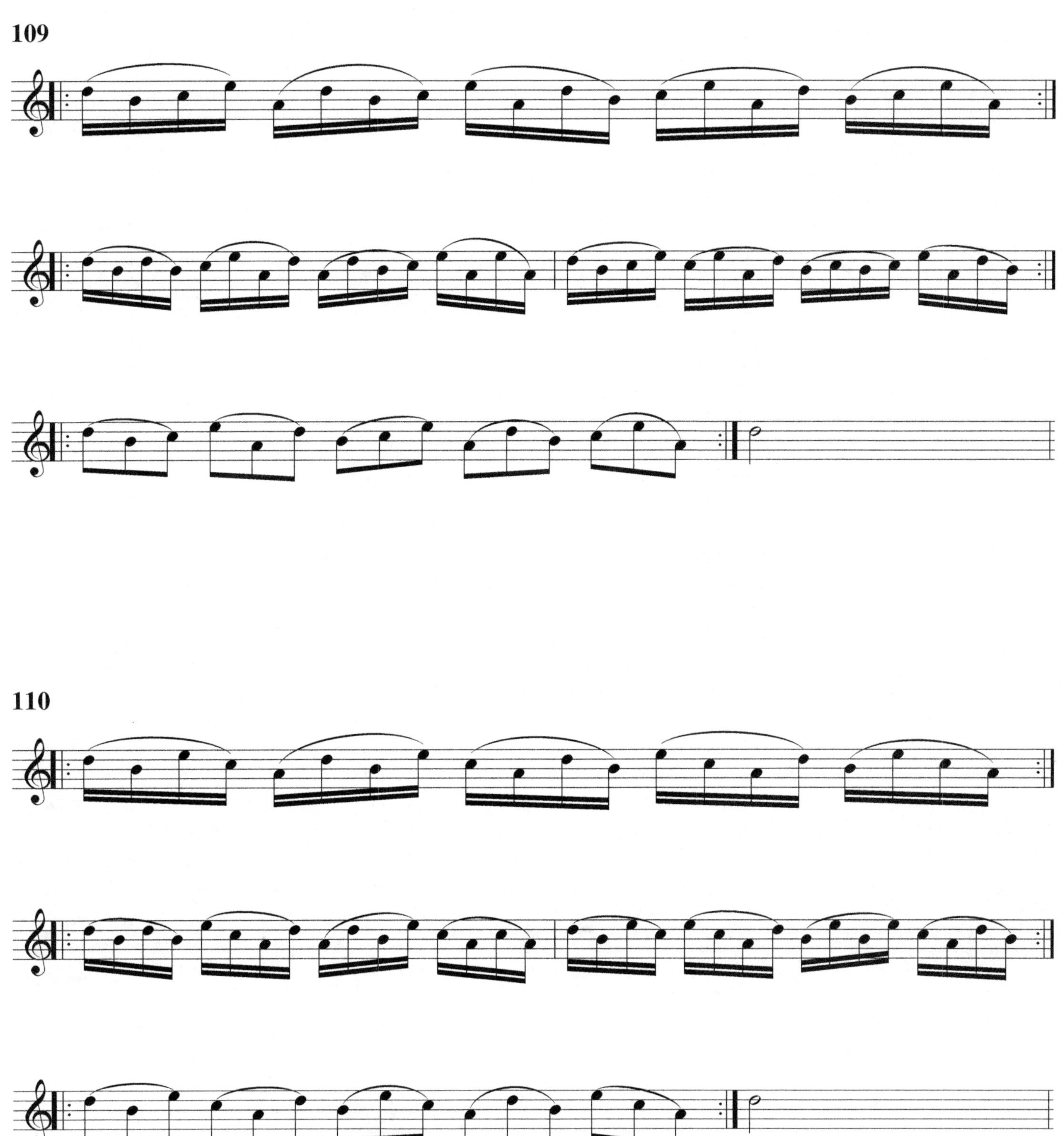

111

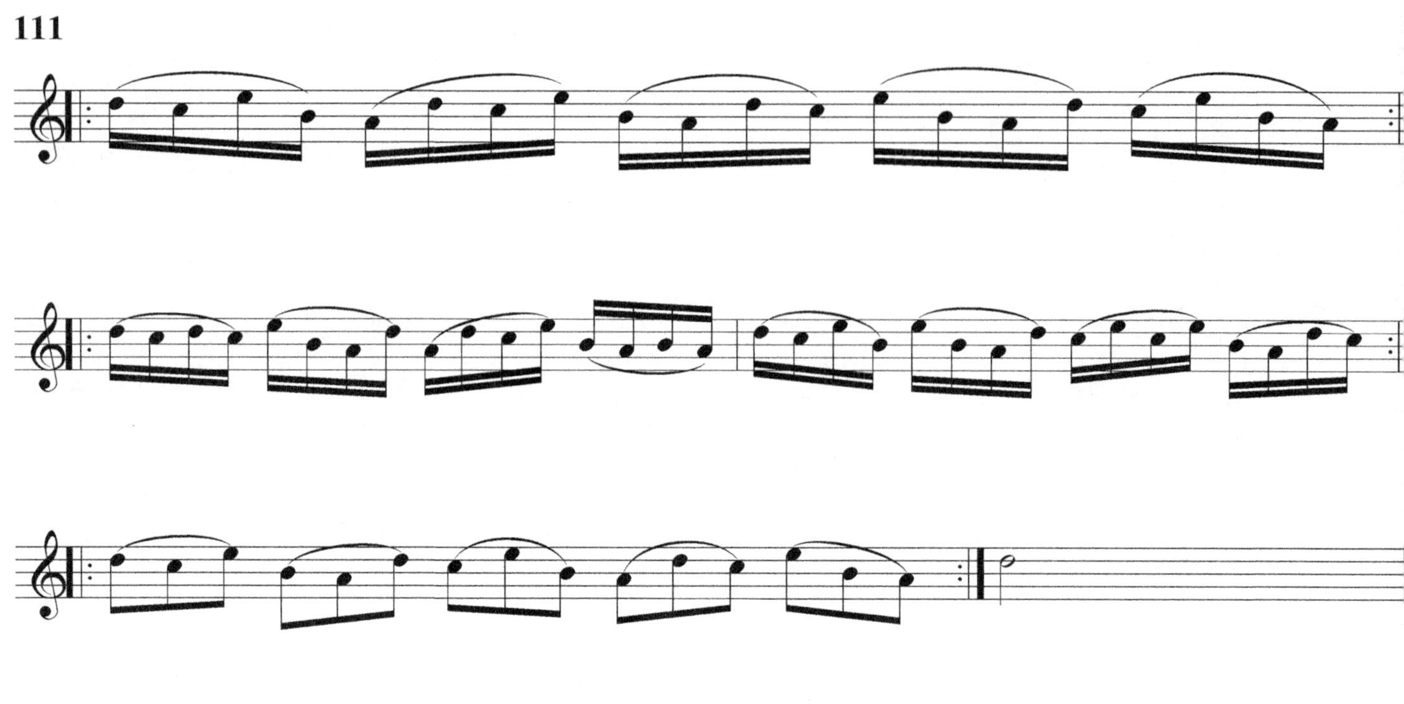

112

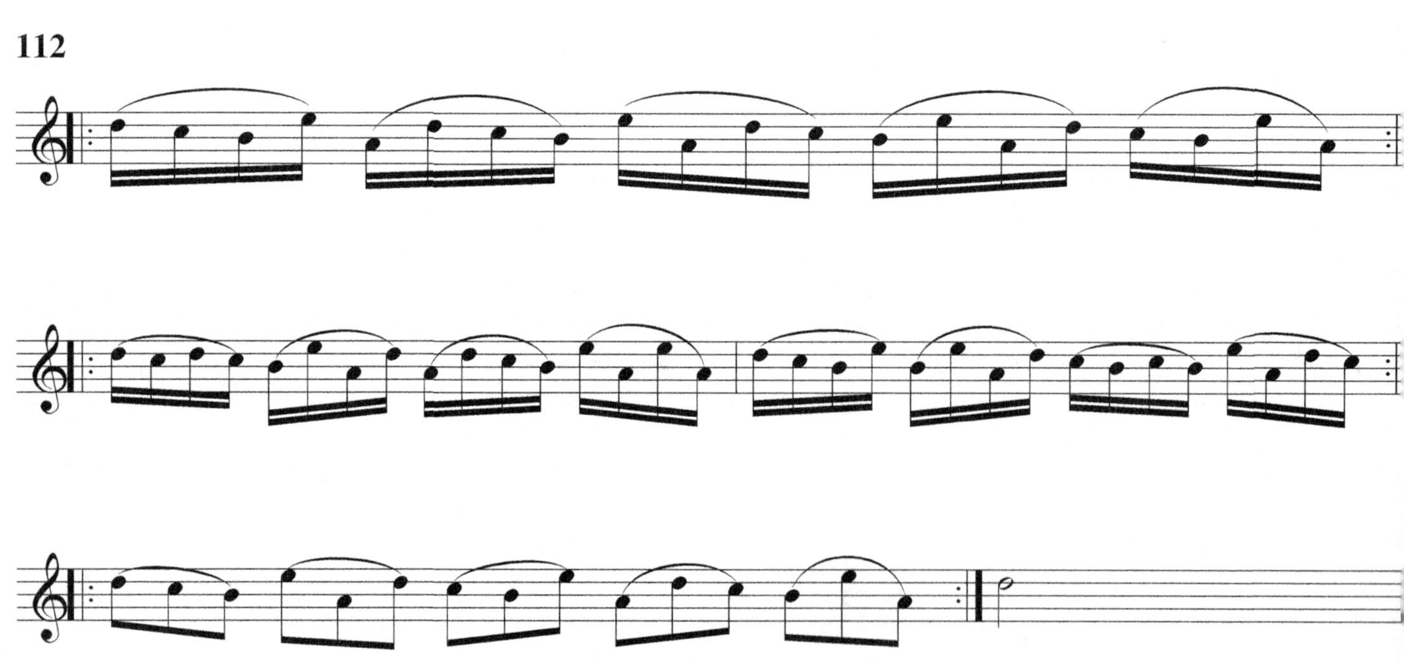

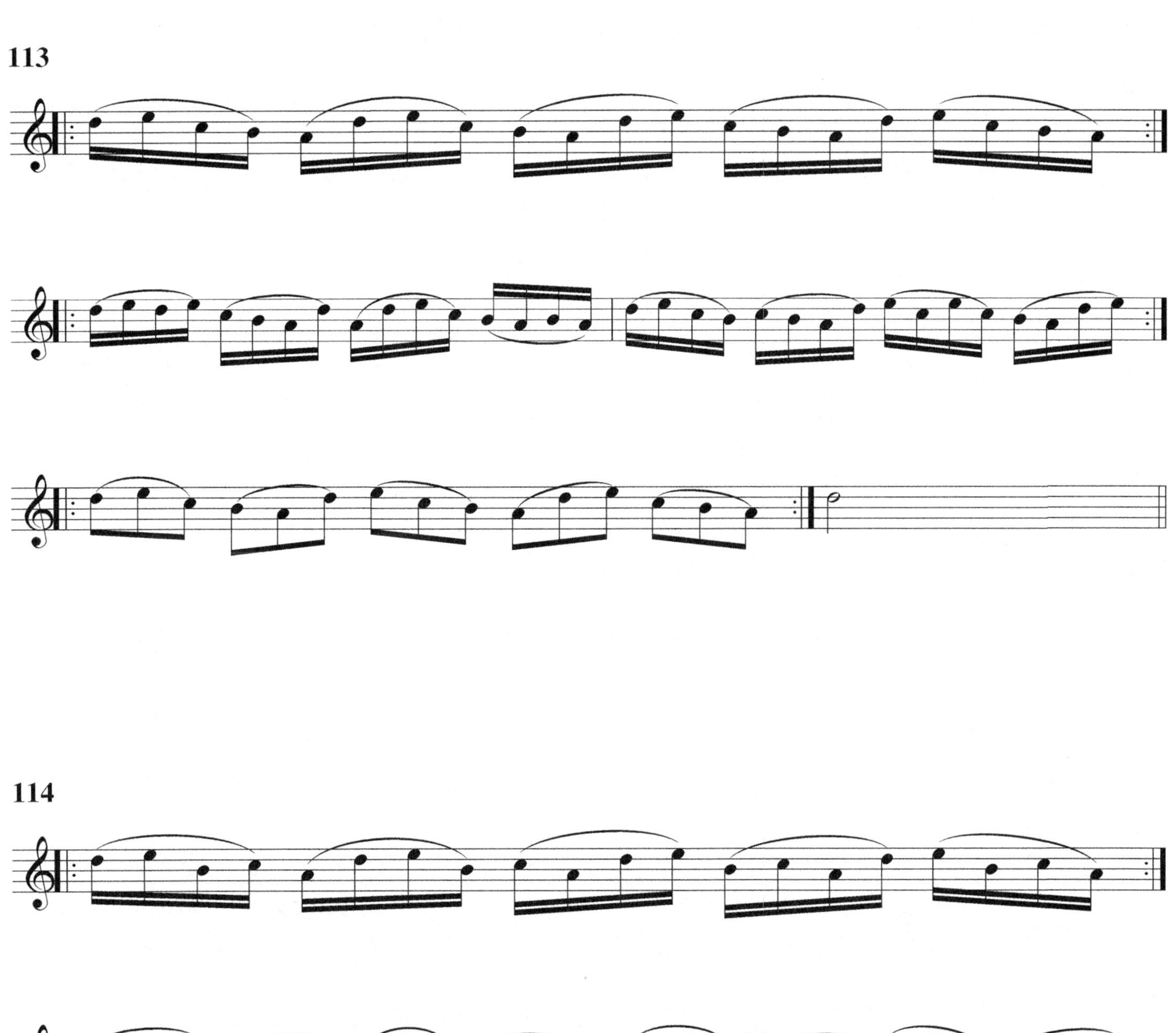

113

114

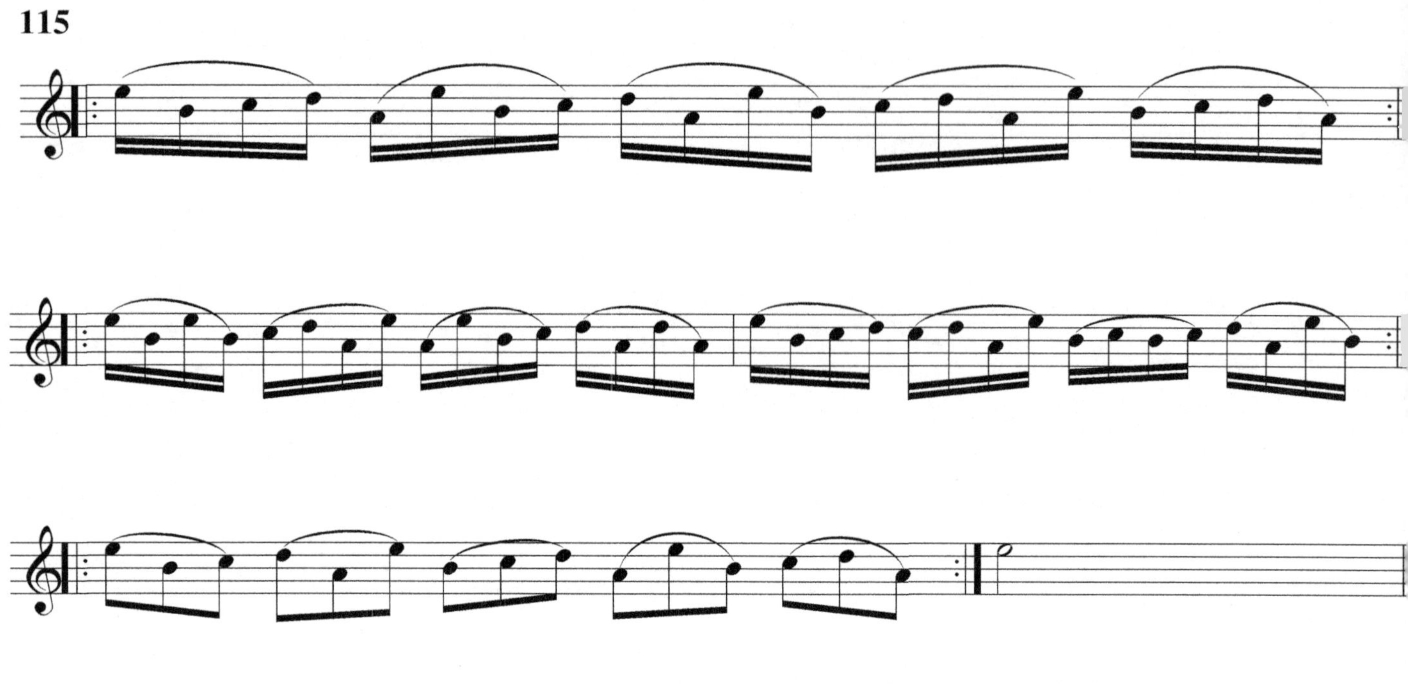

117

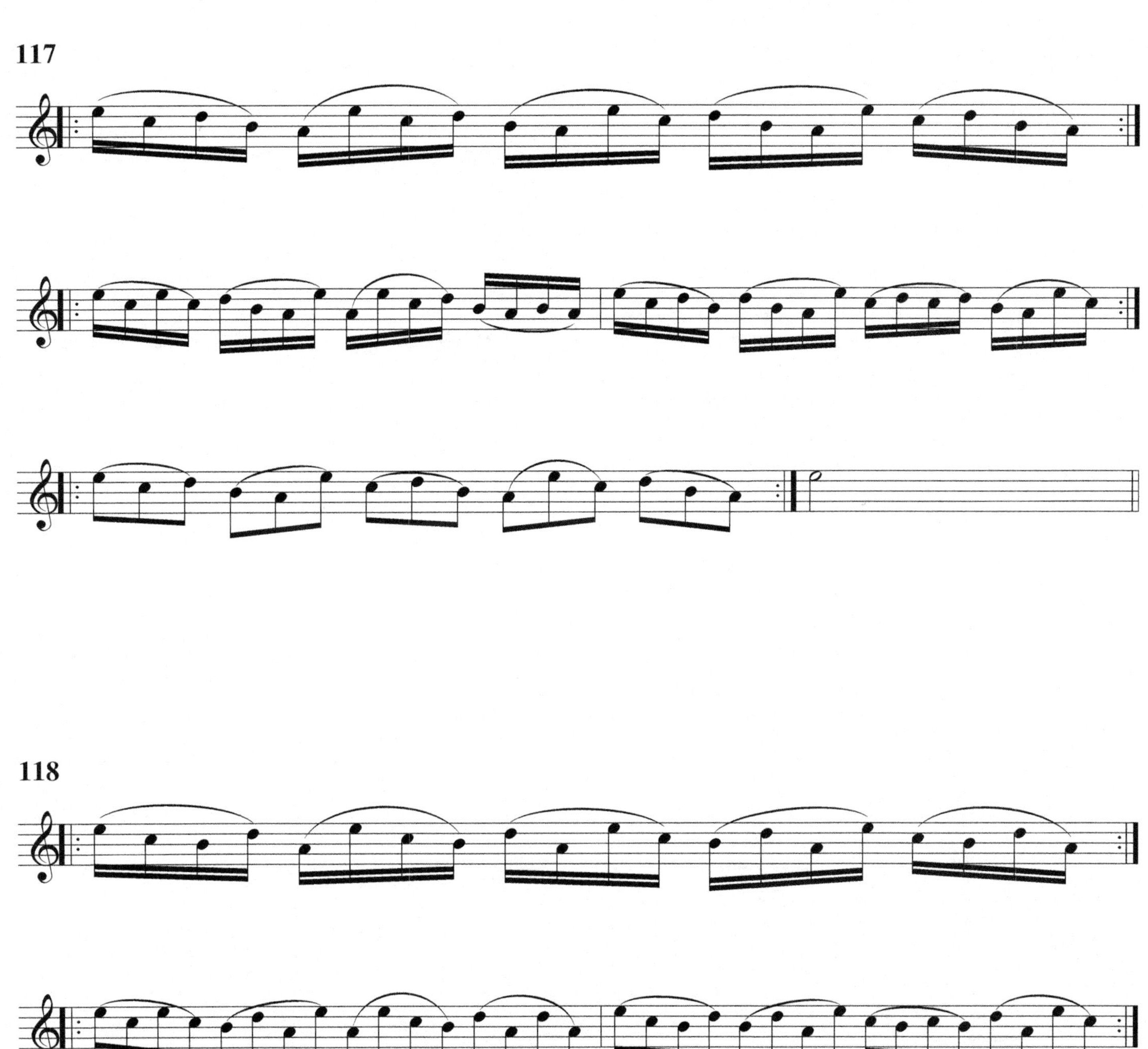

118

119

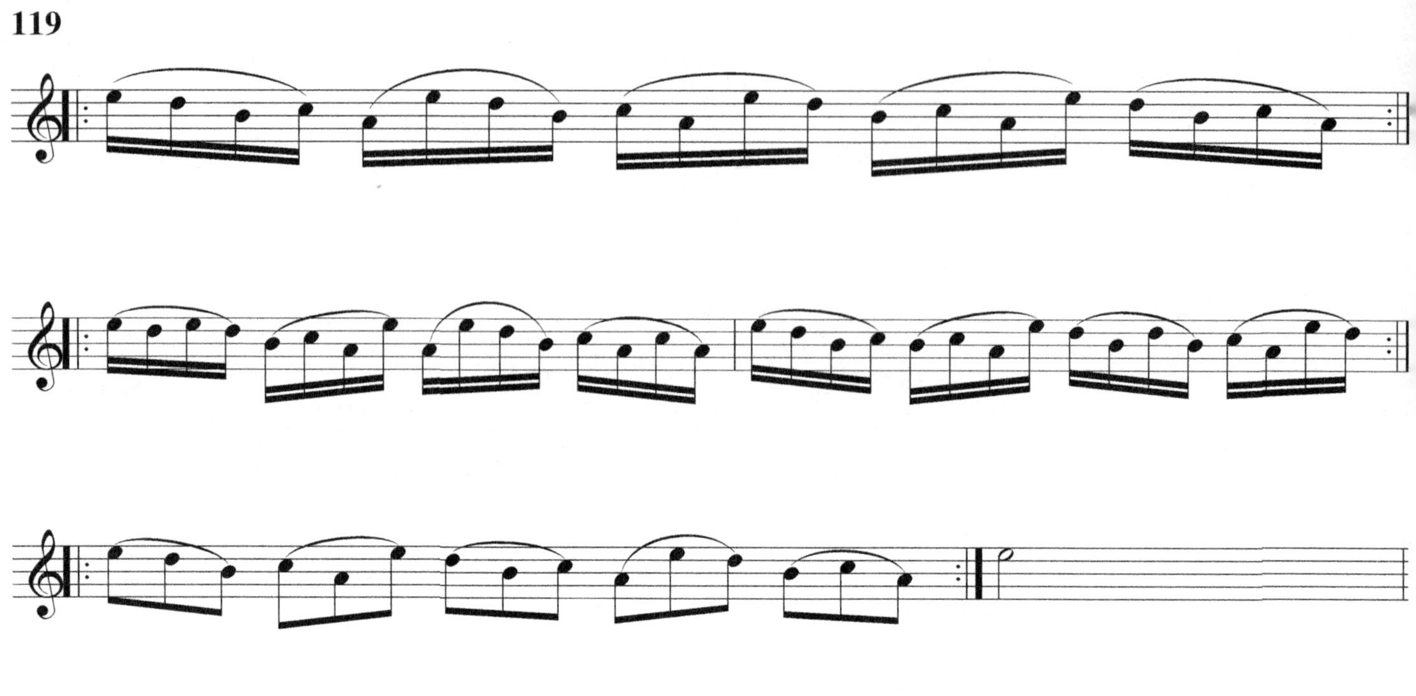

120

Introducing Shifting

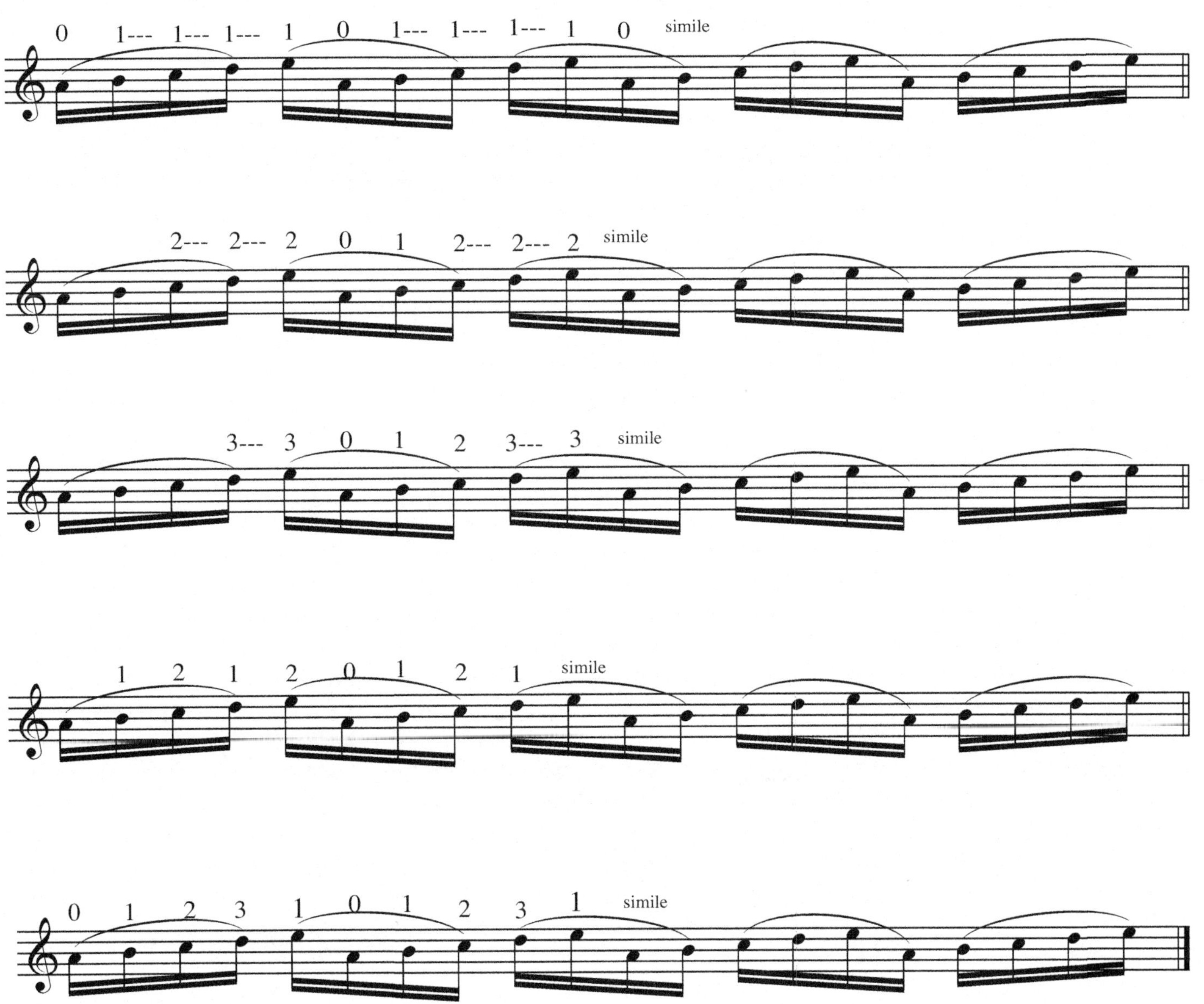

Appendix: How to Use

I. GETTING ACQUAINTED

1. Play as written (choose a "friendly" tempo; use E flat if fourth finger is weak)

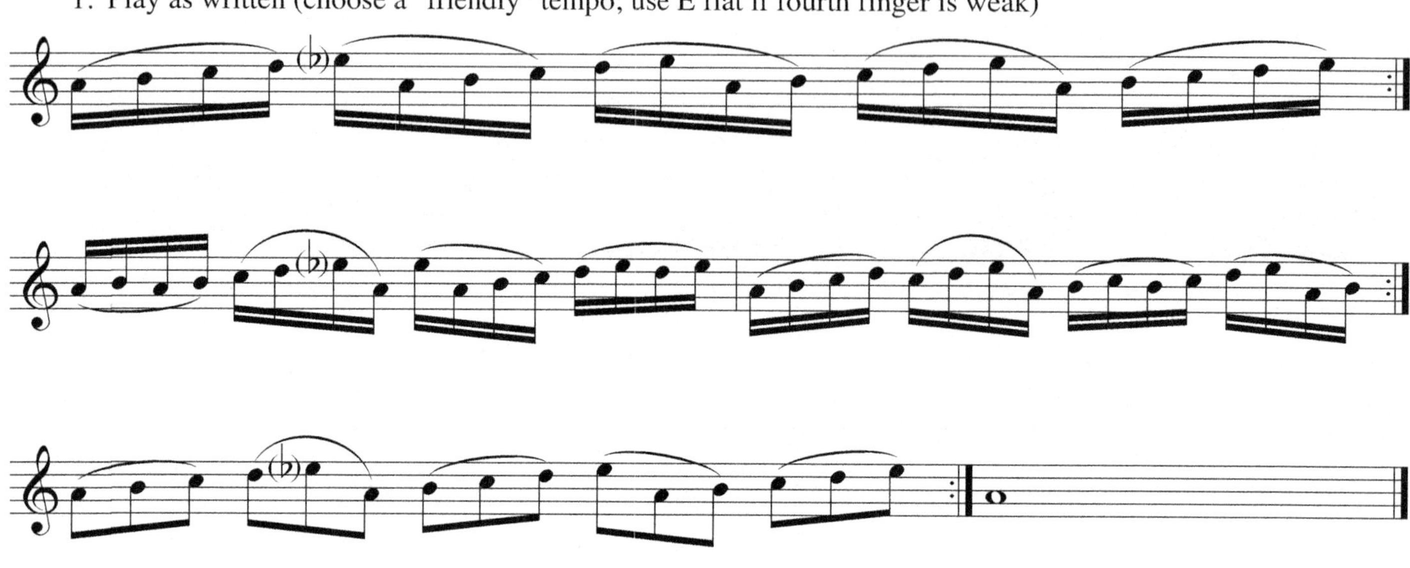

2. "The Long And Short Of It". Play in dotted rhythms (always take repeats)

2. "Meet me in St. Louis". Play first group, then last group, etc...as numbered

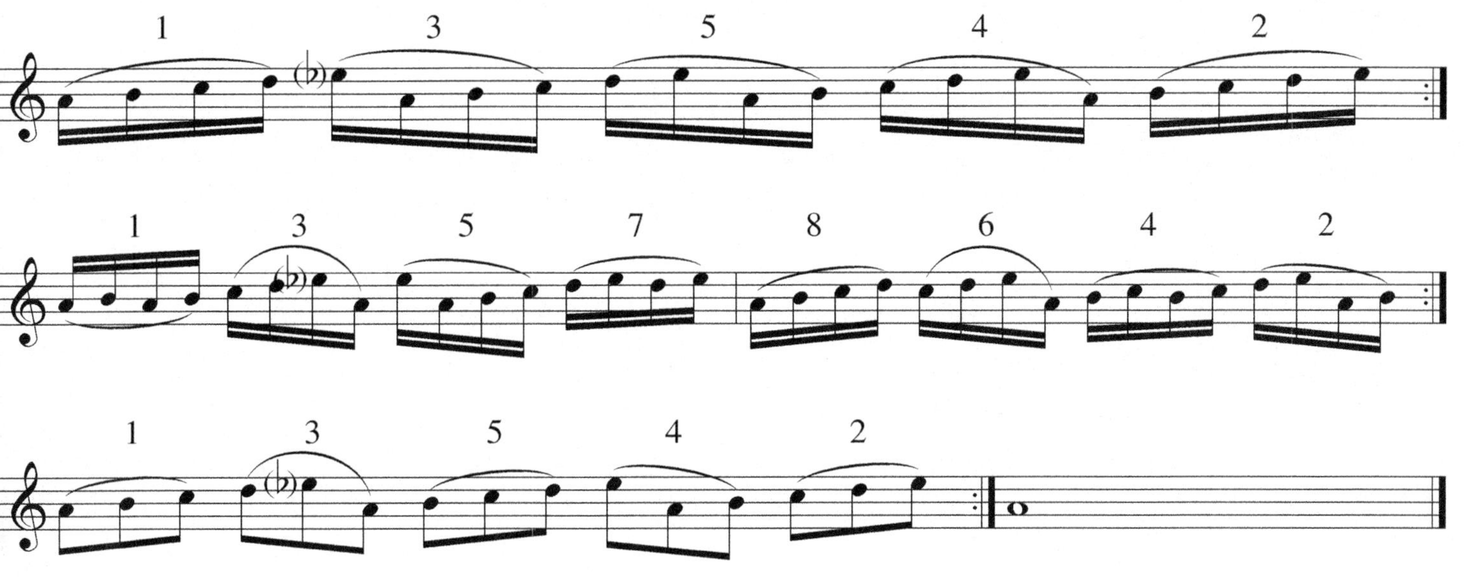

3. "Buddy System" or "The Ruler is King"
A partner holds a ruler over group being played, forcing the eye to read ahead

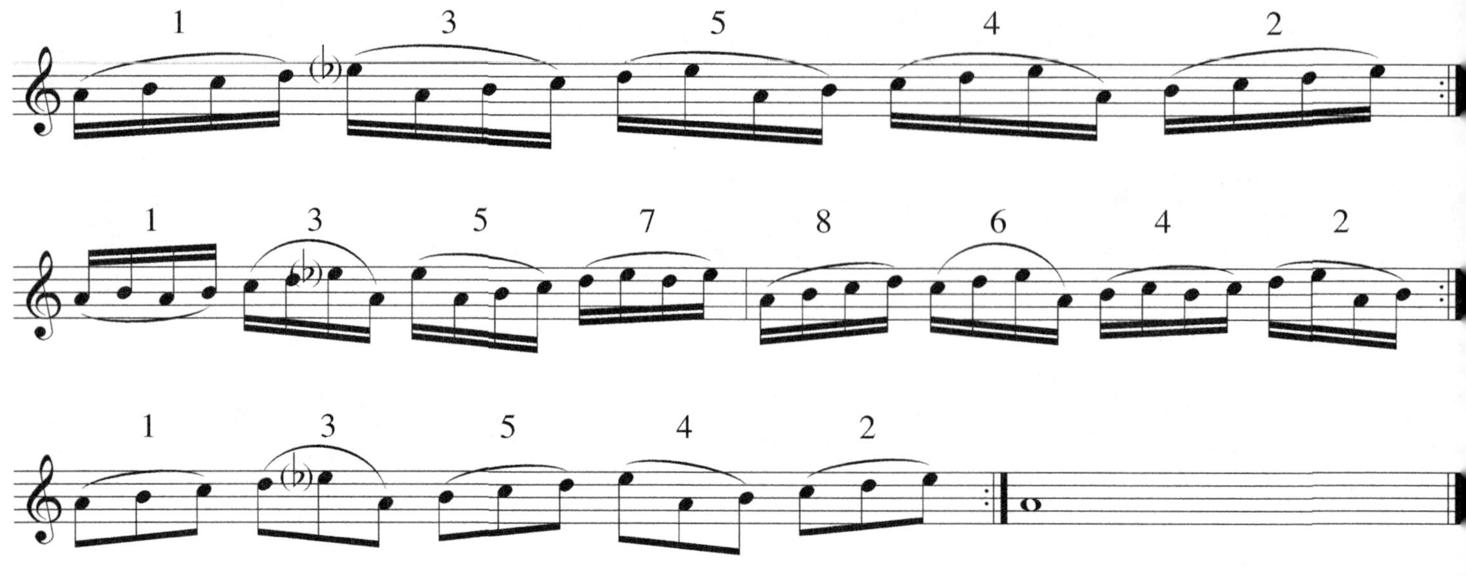

3. "Buddy System" or "The Ruler is King"
A partner holds a ruler over group being played, forcing the eye to read ahead

III. <u>VELOCITY</u>: "Speed Tracks".

1. Find fastest manageable speed. Set metronome 30% faster.
   Practice each beat plus one note.

2. Practicer in groups of 2 beats plus 1 note.

3. Continue adding beats.

4. Find *NEW* fastest manageable speed.

IV. <u>AGILITY</u>

    While doing the above procedures keep the hand loose.
Repeating a phrase such as "loose fingers" often keeps the mind focused.
"Imaging" may help, such as "rubber fingers" or "dancing fingers".

V. <u>FOR A CURVED AND FLEXIBLE FOURTH FINGER</u>

1. As written, but lower the fourth finger a half-step

If the fourth finger will not curve proceed to :
2. Practice in semi-tones

VII. Occasionally practice without shoulder rest--with elbow propped. This will help the independence of fingers and a relaxed 'easy' attutude

 **MEL BAY PUBLICATIONS, INC. • www.MELBAY.com**

UNIQUELY INTERESTING MUSIC!

Printed in Dunstable, United Kingdom